SMALL
LIBRARY
CATALOGING

second edition

by

Herbert H. Hoffman

The Scarecrow Press, Inc.
Metuchen, N.J., & London
1986

Library of Congress Cataloging-in-Publication Data

Hoffman, Herbert H.
  Small library cataloging.

  Includes index.
  1. Cataloging. 2. Classification--Books.
3. Small libraries. I. Title.
Z693.H64 1986   025.3   86-15504
ISBN 0-8108-1910-4

CONTENTS

_____

This book was primarily written for all who find themselves
in charge of a small library without having had the benefit
of formal instruction in library cataloging. The book attempts
to simplify cataloging in small libraries, but it offers no facile
oversimplifications. It does not insult the dedicated layperson's intelligence by pretending that cataloging is easy.

Libraries, even small libraries, are astonishingly complex organizations. There is a proliferation of media. There
are monographs and series and serials, regular and irregular.
There are personal authors and corporate authors, simple and
multiple authors, natural titles and uniform titles, simple and
complex subject headings, and myriad other variables. Library catalogs are complicated structures. There are entry
principles and headings, added entries and analytics, tracings,
location codes, shelf lists, authority files, and much more.

The cataloging rules published by the American Library
Association (ALA) now fill a book of 620 pages. Several books
explaining these rules have been written. It is safe to say
that cataloging remains a specialty mastered by few, even
among librarians with professional degrees. Needless to say,
the volunteering or appointed layperson cannot be expected
to catch up with this growing body of esoteric knowledge in
a few easy lessons. Nor does he or she need to. I claim
that the cataloging of small libraries can safely be simplified.

To this end I propose one major innovation, a deviation
from ALA-style cataloging practice: the principle of title main
entry for all types of publications. This eliminates the traditional distinctions between author, title, and uniform title main
entries with the attendant complications that have made the
ALA cataloging rules so difficult to understand.

Simplified small library cataloging, however, is logically in no way inferior to ALA-style library cataloging. All the concepts and practices introduced in this book, from the description principle to the layout of the catalog card, are based on careful reasoning. Consequently, Small Library Cataloging may not be easy bedside reading. It requires close attention and a motivated reader. But the rewards of studying these chapters will be worth the effort. At the end of the book readers will find many examples for different kinds of publications that may simplify their lives in the library.

Credit for the idea of Small Library Cataloging belongs to Chuck Peterson, custom bookbinder and friend of people who run small libraries. The words, examples, and mistakes contained in these pages, of course, remain the author's responsibility.

Herbert H. Hoffman

INTRODUCTION _____

In the beginning I picture your library as a room full of materials: hardbound and paperbound books, pamphlets, piles
of magazine issues, a large dictionary, an encyclopedia, a few
maps, a box full of audiotapes, some color slides, a rack of
phonograph records, and perhaps even a globe. All of it inherited from an earlier day, none of it cataloged, classified,
or organized for use in any way. Let us say there are also
some shelves, filing cabinets, a desk and chair, a typewriter,
and such. But nothing else. Certainly no manual of proce-
dures.

Or perhaps it is a fairly neat operation. Someone before you had it organized. There is a rudimentary card catalog, some of the books have labels on their spines with numbers typed on them, and several of the magazines have been
bound.

Whatever shape your library is in as you take over,
you will have at least two big questions: What is there to
do? And what should be done first? There are three major
tasks to be done, in this order:

1. Clean up and weeding

2. Organization and arrangement

3. Cataloging

CLEAN UP AND WEEDING

Clean up, here, does not mean dusting and scraping,
although some of that may need to be done, too. What is
meant in this context is the discarding of unwanted items.

A good rule is to discard everything that is not relevant to
the particular purposes your library is to serve. A hospital's
medical library, for example, exists to provide medical information. It does not need a set of Reader's Digest condensed
books, no matter how complete. A church library exists for
the instruction and inspiration of clergy, church school teach-
ers, and members of the congregation. It has no use for
Taylor's Introduction to Linear Algebra or an old volume of
the United States Statutes at Large. An elementary school
library is intended to enhance the reading and discovery skills
of ten-year-olds. It does not need Ernest Jones' Life and
Work of Sigmund Freud, in three volumes. If you find such
treasures but cannot bring yourself to throw the books away
just yet, pack them in cardboard boxes and store them some-
where out of the way. There is nothing wrong with them, as
such. They are merely irrelevant in the present context and
will probably find a better home elsewhere. Maybe they can
be offered to another library or sold at a book sale.

There is another class of irrelevant books that should
be discarded: old books and old editions. A book entitled
So You are Going to College: A Guide for Students, dated
1923, is not likely to help today's young people prepare for
their academic future. My advice: throw it away. Don't
waste time and space cataloging such materials. Or take the
sixth edition of Introduction to Biochemistry. The library
has the ninth edition on the shelf, and the tenth is on order.
My advice: throw the sixth edition away. It is probably a
gift occasioned by someone else's housecleaning.

Duplicates, too, must be carefully evaluated. Sometimes
they are needed. If a certain book is in constant demand, a
gift copy would be most welcome. You may even buy a second
copy. But more often than not one copy of a book is plenty.
Duplicates must be justified for they take away space and ab-
sorb processing time. Very seldom should you accept a third
copy of anything. If you are given four copies of a new book
(new to the library, that is) that looks relevant, pick the two
best looking specimens and throw or give the others away.

Some of the things you find may be very relevant to
your library but consist of incomplete sets--an encyclopedia
without the index volume, for example, or perhaps a run of
magazines from 1950 to 1960. It is a good idea to set aside
such incomplete sets and hold on to them until everything else

has been put in order. Sometimes missing volumes miraculously
reappear, or two or three independent gifts combine to form a
complete run of back issues of a desirable magazine.

Having discarded unwanted materials and set aside incomplete and doubtful ones, you are ready for the second
task.

ORGANIZING

It is obvious that books, periodicals, cassettes, slides,
and all other information media kept in the library must be put
away according to some plan. That library is best in which
things can be expected to be in certain places. The design
of a good library organization plan presupposes a clear understanding of a number of principles derived primarily from the
structural characteristics of the media stored in the library.
It also requires a knowledge of the reasons and methods for
grouping different kinds of library media apart from others
and of the ways of arranging documents within their groups.
Part I of this book, therefore, deals with questions of library
organization in terms of the structure of publications, files of
library materials, classification, shelf arrangement, and the
marking of books. When that work is done and your books
are on their shelves you are ready for the third task.

CATALOGING

For purposes of this book, cataloging means preparing
library catalog cards and their orderly arrangement in a catalog cabinet. To be effective, the resulting index to the collection must be clear, consistent, and comprehensive. Part II
of this book is devoted to the logical principles that govern
cataloging and to practical questions such as description principle, what goes into a bibliographic record, main entry, added
entries and their headings, and filing rules.

Throughout this book it is assumed that readers are
laypersons who will want to make their own cataloging decisions and prepare their own catalog cards, either on conven-
tional typewriters or on word processing computers. In the
event that a reader will utilize printed catalog cards for some
books, an appendix has been added explaining the slightly

different card layout practiced by the Library of Congress. Also shown are typical examples of CIP (Cataloging in Publication), printed bibliographic aids, online aids, and the MARC (machine readable cataloging) format.

PART I:

ARRANGEMENT OF PUBLICATIONS
ON THE SHELF

Chapter 1

STRUCTURE OF PUBLICATIONS _____

Writing for laypeople in charge of small libraries, one is tempted to simplify things and begin by saying that library work is the art of arranging books for use. This is a good statement, and it is true. But it does not say much. It does not even allow for the fact that, first of all, we must define what we mean by "books."

WHAT IS A BOOK?

Traditionally, books were sheets of paper bound together between covers, forming containers for someone's printed words. But today not all words that are recorded are stored as print on paper between covers, and not all those that are in print on paper are bound as books. Many words are recorded in spoken form on discs or on tape, or in printed form reduced to microfilm, or typed on single sheets and stapled. There are pamphlets, loose-leaf sets, periodicals, technical reports, films, and many other media designed for the storage of information. Modern libraries house them all and keep them ready for use.

All of these information storage media can be said to be books in the general sense, while only some of them are print-on-paper books in the special sense. To remove the ambiguity from cataloging terminology, library textbooks and manuals nowadays avoid the term book altogether, speaking instead of items, documents, and works. But the terminology has not been standardized. To make it clear what we are discussing, we must carefully define these three terms.

3

First, a "work." The ALA Glossary of Library and Information Science (Chicago, American Library Association,
1983) defines a work as a defined body of recorded information, as distinct from the substance on which it is recorded.
This definition can be expanded: a work is a unit of someone's intellectual, scholarly, or artistic creation. Examples
of works, for our purposes here, are an essay, a story, a
novel, a poem, a play, a theoretical treatise, an article, a
paper, or a lecture.

The second term is "document." The ALA Glossary defines a document as a physical entity on which a work is recorded or on which several works or parts of works are recorded. As examples the glossary lists books and sound recordings, among other types. A document, then, is any physical storage unit, of any medium, that contains one or more
works of recorded information.

To emphasize the distinction between a work and a document, we may want to consider a lecture. If it is published
as print on paper it may appear as a book. But if it is published recorded on tape it may appear as a cassette. The
book and the cassette are different documents. But the lecture is the same work in both cases.

The word "item," finally, has several meanings. In
cataloging, the ALA GLOSSARY states, item means bibliographic
item. A bibliographic item is defined as a document or a set
of documents treated as an entity and as such forming the
basis for a single bibliographic description. In other words,
an item can be either a single-document item or a multi-
document item. Most novels (works) appear in books (documents) that are published as one physical volume (single-
document item). But a large treatise may be one work published in two volumes. This would be a two-document item.

To make these distinctions clearer, here are some further examples. The book you are holding in your hand is an
item, one bibliographic unit. It is also a document, one physical unit. And as it happens, it contains one sole work. This
is the simplest kind of item there is. It can be described by
a formula as follows:

                    1 ITEM, 1 DOCUMENT, 1 WORK

But not all items are that simply structured. On occasion a writer produces a work that, on publication, fills two books. The formula for such a work would be this:

1 ITEM, 2 DOCUMENTS, 1 WORK

Some publications contain many different works. A one-volume anthology, for example, may hold eighty poems. This would be the formula:

1 ITEM, 1 DOCUMENT, 80 WORKS

Or consider a set of phonograph records that contain twelve pieces of music on three discs. Here is the formula:

1 ITEM, 3 DOCUMENTS, 12 WORKS

Clearly, books or items, containers of recorded information, come in many different formats. But there is an underlying order to this world of publications. Given the definitions of work, document, and item shown above we can agree on the following formulation:

> All items cataloged in a library consist of one or more documents and contain one or more works.

It seems, then, that there are at least eight major structural types of items that all require slightly different treatment in cataloging. The chart on page 6 demonstrates these eight item types.

If all books were simple stand-alone works of type 1, each written by one author, the rules for classifying and cataloging books could be reduced to a one-page statement. But the structural diversity introduces an element of choice into the work of arranging books on the shelves. While some books come as single-volume items and can stand either here or there, others come in sets of two or more volumes. Some multi-volume sets must stand together, while others can be treated either as sets in one location or as so many individual volumes dispersed in different locations.

Consider a set of two volumes, an item consisting of two documents. Each volume contains a dozen essays by different authors. Volume 1 deals with American politics, volume

			One work per document	More than one work per document	Multi-document item holds one work
Item consists of only one document			1	2	
Item consists of two or more documents	Closed item	Document titles as well as item title	3	4	
		Item title only		5	8
	Open item	Document titles as well as item title		6	
		Item title only		7	

2 with European politics. If it is an item of type 4, the set might best be split up so that volume 1 can stand with all other books on American politics and volume 2 with all other books on European politics. But if it is an item of type 5, the set must stay together.

From the point of view of the library user, the proper arrangement of books may spell the difference between finding and not finding required information. In fact, these decisions are crucial since the whole purpose of running a library is, of course, to facilitate the retrieval of stored information.

EXAMPLES

Here are a few schematics to exemplify different types of items. The first is a single-document item:

Urinary analysis and diagnosis
by Louis Heinzelmann.

It is an item consisting of one document. The entire contents of this item is one work. Since the book contains one work and stands alone, is not part of any set, one could call it a stand-alone work. It is a book of type 1. In such books the title of the item is also the title of the work contained in it. This is the most common type of book.

The following example is an item that looks different but is also of type 1:

Symphony No. 2 in D
by Johannes Brahms.

This item also consists of one document. It also contains one
work. The title of the disc is also the title of the work recorded on it. In terms of medium we distinguish between
a phonograph record and a book, of course. But structurally
there is no difference between these two examples. The same
cataloging principles apply, or should apply, to all items of
type 1.

This book, too, stands alone. And it is an item of one
document. But it contains essays or chapters by thirty-eight
physicians, a total of sixty-three works. It is a book of
type 2:

Concepts of disease
ed. by Joel G. Brunson
and Edward A. Gall.

Notice that the title of this item is not the title of any of
the works in it. Each of the sixty-three works has its own
title. The reader will appreciate the difficulties of a library
user trying to locate one of these works. Impossible, unless
the library takes steps to point them out by indexing them.

Here is an example of a multi-document item:

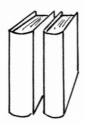

Advances in librarianship
ed. by Melvin J. Voigt.

These two volumes form the beginning of an open set of books,
an annual series. Each book in the set contains numerous
works. It is a set of type 7. This set must stay together
in one location because the individual documents have no titles
of their own.

Here is a closed set of two volumes that contains only one work. It is an item of type 8:

Climatology
by Arnold Becker
and Joe Doe.

Becker and Doe together wrote the whole book or, more precisely, the whole work which grew so large that it filled a set of two books. The entire set, of course, stands together in one location and the work title is the same as the item title.

These two volumes also form a closed set of two books:

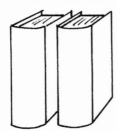

Socialism and American life
ed. by Donald Drew Egbert
and Stow Persons.

They contain contributions by a dozen writers, a total of fifteen works, each with its own distinctive work title. It is an item of type 5. Since there are no individual document titles, the set stands together under its item title.

Sets of two or more volumes sometimes consist of individually titled documents. Here is an example of an open set of type 6:

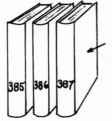

The sixties: radical change in
American religion
ed. by James M. Gustafson.
Vol. 387 of Annals of the American
Academy of Political and Social
Science, January 1970.

Each of the numbered volumes in this item bears a different
document title. Each of the books in the set deals with a
different topic. Such a set may be broken up so that each
book can be placed with others on its subject. But of course
the set can also be left standing together, which requires
a totally different classification and cataloging job.

These examples demonstrate the complexities of the
structure of publications. Unless we clearly differentiate
between an item, a document, and a work, we shall find it
difficult to talk about organizing "books" in libraries, let
alone about classifying and cataloging them.

Chapter 2

FILES, SHELF ARRANGEMENT, AND
CLASSIFICATION _____

FILES

A file, in the context of a library, is simply a location, a
place for books and other publications. Some files consist
of cabinets filled with manila folders; some files are trays
holding microfilm reels or filmstrips. Most library materials
are housed on shelves. Thus, the entire stack area where
the bulk of the books are kept is a file. If some shelves
have been set aside for often-used reference books, these
reference shelves are another file. It is not unusual even for
small libraries to have a dozen different files.

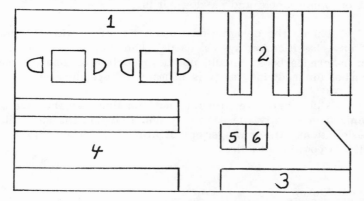

The above illustration shows the floor plan of a fictitious
library where the materials are stored in six different files.
To distinguish the files from each other they are given names.
The six files in this hypothetical library have been named as

follows: (1) Current periodicals; (2) Back issues; (3) Reference books; (4) Stacks; (5) Map case; and (6) Dictionary
stand.

File Designations

Since the books that belong into the several files often
have to be marked on the spines the corresponding catalog
cards likewise have to be marked, and since the names of the
files are somewhat long, abbreviated file designations are
usually adopted.   Thus, a file reserved for very large books
may be called OVERSIZE, or perhaps FOLIO (a designation
inherited from the printing industry of an earlier day), or
simply F.   A file set aside for reference books is often designated by REF or perhaps R.   And so on.   While the choice
of a file designation is an arbitrary act, a few principles can
be stated.   First, the designation should, if possible, be
self-explanatory.   Thus, the designation REF or even R is
better, and says more, than a green dot.

Second, the designation should be as small as is possible.
A file used to store atlases and maps should not be designated
GEOGRAPHICAL ATLASES AND MAPS.   The short word
ATLAS is better.   One must remember that designations must
fit on spine labels and catalog cards.

Third, the designation must not conflict with the notation
of any classification system used.   The file designation R
for reference books should not be used if R is also the class
symbol for medicine, as it is in many college libraries.

While there are probably not two libraries that are organized in exactly the same way and that use the same file
designations, the arrangement of library materials into many
files is common practice.

Open Files

Some files are directly and freely accessible to all library
users.   The great majority of files in American libraries are
open files.

Closed Files

Closed or controlled files are files to which only library personnel have direct access. In a small library there will be few closed files. A possible example would be a file of slides arranged by a homemade system of codes that are meaningless to the library user. For efficient retrieval and to insure proper placement of returned slides the file might be restricted, to be serviced only by the librarian.

SHELF ARRANGEMENT

Fixed Location

Publications can be arranged within their files in many ways. In former times books were often arranged on shelves in a fixed location. A book marked 18/3, for example, was the third book from the left on shelf number 18. Fixed location shelving is not used much today, if at all, because it lacks hospitality, the ability to accommodate future insertions. When the shelf is full there is no way to insert a new book or a second copy between book 18/3 and book 18/4.

Accession Order

A modified fixed location order that is still used in many files today is the arrangement of publications on the shelves in the order of their arrival in the library. Each book is given an accession number as it is acquired and is filed by that number. The 117th book acquired will thus stand to the right of the 116th book. It will be followed by the 118th book, and so on, regardless of who wrote it and what it is about. This system, of course, has the same faults as the fixed location system: it disperses multiple copies of the same book, and different books on the same subject, more or less widely from each other.

Numerical Order

Some types of documents come equipped with a built-in system of numbers. For example, the California Division of

Mines and Geology publishes at irregular intervals a series
of "Special Reports" on different topics; these reports are
numbered, beginning with SR 1 (1950). Another example is
the Conference Board of New York, an independent business
research organization; their periodically issued reports are
numbered at the source and are cross-indexed by report numbers in an annual cumulative subject index. Serial publications of this type abound in many types of libraries. They
are best kept together in one shelf section, arranged by their
own numbers. This makes the librarian's work easier and it
also guarantees easy retrieval.

Alphabetical Order

        Some files, such as periodical back issues, can be kept
in order alphabetically by title. An issue of the Nation, for
example, can be clearly identified as such from the cover and
placed between Modern Age and Oceans. If enough space is
left between titles, alphabetical arrangement allows for the
insertion of multiple copies and successive issues of the same
title as well as for the addition of new titles. It is a hospi-
table system for arranging publications that carry an easily
visible name on the outside, such as magazines, maps, or
certain pamphlet series. However, alphabetical order does
not keep together publications that treat the same subject.
Only classified arrangement will accomplish this.

CLASSIFICATION

        By far the best known method of arranging books on
library shelves is classification. Every American child is
familiar with the decimal classification system, for example,
which for many, under the name of "the Dewey system,"
has become a synonym for library classification in general.

        The principle of book classification is simple enough:
every book is assigned a relative position on the shelf according to a salient characteristic. This leads to the grouping
of like publications within a file. There are many possible
criteria for grouping. The best known is classification by
subject.

Subject Classification

This refers to the grouping of publications within a file according to their main subject. A certain medical book, for example, may contain one sole work about human anatomy and fit neatly into the class "Anatomy." Another book deals with human physiology and fits into the class "Physiology." When all like books are assigned consistently to these two classes, all books containing works on anatomy and all those on physiology will eventually stand together. This is the essence of subject classification.

But knowledge recorded in books and other types of publications is not restricted to such simple and clear-cut topics. In the field of mental health, for example, there is a class "Psychology" (BF in the Library of Congress classification system; 150 in the Dewey Decimal classification system) and a closely related class "Psychiatry" (LC: RC 454; DC: 616.89). Since a book can stand in only one place, a decision must be made for every book. It takes expertise about the subject to do that properly. Consider a book such as James Covington Coleman's Abnormal Psychology and Modern Life. Since the title contains the word "psychology," a layperson might class this book in psychology. The expert, however, knows that it belongs with the books in psychiatry.

Also, many topics can be logically subdivided. In psychiatry we have books on neuroses and books on psychoses, for example. The books on psychoses may deal with functional psychoses or with organic psychoses. Books about functional psychoses may deal with schizophrenia or with paranoia, and so forth. The possible divisions are almost infinite, and to determine authoritatively whether a given book such as Betrayal of the Body, by Alexander Lowen, should stand with other books on schizophrenia or with those on paranoia, or perhaps elsewhere, is no easy task.

It does not become easier if we consider that there are also collections of works. A certain book may hold, say, ten works, each about a certain well-defined topic. The book itself, being just the "empty container"--the term comes from a recently published glossary issued by the Educational Resources Information Center (ERIC)--has no subject at all. But each of the works in it has a different subject. To which subject area shall the item be assigned?

Nor does classification become easier if we add to these considerations the fact that works can deal with more than one topic simultaneously, either hierarchically related to a broader subject or not, as well as with several different relationships between topics, such as mental health and social class, mental health in a historical perspective, or mental health as an aspect of abnormal psychology.

Needless to say, the subtleties of subject classification often baffle even the experienced librarian. It is easy to find examples of inconsistency in the output of no lesser library than that of the United States Congress. In that library two unrelated books stand near to each other-- Social statistics and the city (HA29) and Statistical methods applied to experiments in agriculture and biology (HA 40)-- while Beyer's Handbook of tables for probability and statistics (QA276), closely related to the second book, stands far apart from it.

Clearly, the assignment of books to their proper places in a classification system is not a task for the unprepared. It seems naive to expect lay personnel placed in charge of small libraries to classify books as if there were nothing to it. Yet in practice that is exactly what usually happens. Administrators simply expect that the collection will be cataloged (often confusing "classification" with "cataloging"), and that will be that. A compromise solution to the dilemma must be found.

Let's first discuss a few key terms.

Classes

Library classification systems are more or less carefully developed schedules of hierarchically related categories. They all attempt the same thing: to compartmentalize the complete body of knowledge within their scope in a logical fashion so that like books in the fields covered can be placed side by side on the shelves. A book thus compartmentalized is said to belong to a certain class.

Notations

Books and catalog cards must be marked so that they can be kept in order and retrieved. The names of classes

are usually too long to fit in the available space on the spine
of books and on catalog cards. It would be far too cumbersome to label a book, "Diseases of the cardiovascular system," which is one of the classes in the Dewey system.
Instead, a so-called notation is introduced consisting
of arbitrarily assigned short symbols that represent the long
names of classes. In the Dewey system, the book on diseases
of the cardiovascular system would belong to the class "616.1";
in the Library of Congress system it might belong to class
"RC 669"; and in the system of the National Library of Medicine the proper notation would be "WG 100."

Dewey Decimal Classification

The best known of the published classification systems
is the decimal classification devised by Melvil Dewey one century ago. The Dewey system divides knowledge into ten
arbitrarily established main classes presented in the following
order:

    0 Generalities
    1 Philosophy
    2 Religion
    3 Social sciences
    4 Language
    5 Pure sciences
    6 Technology
    7 Arts
    8 Literature
    9 Geography and history

Each of the ten main classes is divided into ten "divisions."
The main class "Religion," for example, is divided as follows:

    20 Religion in general
    21 Natural religion
    22 Bible
    23 Christian doctrinal theology
    24 Christian moral theology
    25 Christian pastoral theology
    26 Christian social theology
    27 History of Christian Church
    28 Christian denominations
    29 Other religions

Note that a second digit was added to main class 2, Religion.
It designates the division. Thus 22 means "main Class 2
Division 2," defined as "Bible." The resulting one hundred
divisions are further subdivided into ten sections each. This
means that a third digit is added to the main class and the
division digits. The division "Bible," for example, is spread
into ten sections as follows:

220 Bible in general
221 Old Testament
222 Historical books
223 Poetic books
224 Prophetic books
225 New Testament
226 Gospels and acts
227 Epistles
228 Revelation or Apocalypse
229 Apocrypha, pseudepigrapha, etc.

Each of the sections is represented by a three digit number.
Thus, if we include "000," a total of 1,000 sections result.

Each section can be further subdivided as needed by
adding decimals to the three digit section number. In this
way, for the long topic "Adaptation of animals to meteorological factors," a brief notation is substituted: 591.54. Catalogers refer to this kind of number as a "class" number or
"Dewey" number.

In many cases it is possible to add decimal digits to
base numbers according to seven mnemonic tables. Mnemonic
(i.e., memorable, easy to remember) here means that the
same combination of numbers always signifies the same attri-
bute or characteristic. The table of standard subdivisions,
for example, allows the combination of a subject base number
like 591.54 with a standard subdivision like -09 for geographical or historical treatment. The resulting number, 591.5409,
presumably stands for a book that treats geographically (or
historically) the adaptation of animals to meteorological factors.

Another mnemonic table provides digits that stand for
areas. Thus, -6 stands for Africa. Added to the standard
subdivision -09, a number like this could result: 591.54096,
for "adaptation of African animals to meteorological factors."

Although biography can hardly be called an "area,"
one area division, -2, is nevertheless very useful. If added
to the standard subdivision -09 it makes a handy device for
collecting all biographies in a subject class together. Thus,
if theology carries the Dewey number 230, then biographies
of theologians are in 230.92.

The entire classification system, now in the 19th edition,
is available for purchase in three volumes from Forest Press,
Inc., Albany, New York. The system is used in thousands of
general libraries in America.

Abridged Dewey Classification

There is an abridged version of the decimal system,
also designed for general libraries (libraries that cover all
subjects from philosophy to science and art). The abridged
version provides fewer but broader classes with shorter notations. A book dealing with animal adaptation to meteorological factors would be placed into the subsection 591.5 (animal ecology).

Paradoxical as it sounds, for a small special collection
concentrating on detailed aspects of a narrow subject area
the abridged version is less suitable than the full Dewey
classification because it results in all books falling into a few
broad classes. In a technical library dealing with the de-
sulfuration, storage, mechanical treatment, and physical
properties of coal, for example, all books would stand in the
same subsection 662.6 for "Coal." In many cases, then, using
the abridged Dewey classification would be equivalent to no
classification at all.

Applying the Decimal Classification

The Dewey tables are not completely logical. Like all
other classification systems, the Dewey system must struggle
with interrelationships of knowledge that are so complex that
it may not be possible to maintain a clearly logical system.
A book on the theory of corporate financial reporting (655.3)
stands right next to a completely unrelated directory of book
and periodical publishers (655.4). The literature of Romance
languages goes into 879.9, but the literature of one Romance
language, Catalan, is placed elsewhere, in 849.9. The number
for the whole of the Old Testament (221) is on the same level

as the number for the historical books of the Bible (222),
but those books, being a subdivision of the Old Testament,
should logically be subdivisions of 221.

Time divisions and topical divisions of a subject are
often in conflict. Thus there is a section 723 for medieval
architecture (a time division) and a section 726 for church
buildings (a topical division). There is no convenient slot
for medieval churches.

The extensive analytical index presents hundreds of
alphabetized, and therefore logically unrelated, terms in a
terse, telescopic style. The index might list specific sub-
topics under a broader topic, but gives no hint how to find
a number for a book that deals with the broad topic in general.

Public opinion notwithstanding, the use of the Dewey
classification is not simple but quite difficult. No shortcuts
can be offered here. However, several articles and books
have been written on the application of the Dewey system,
two recent ones being An Introduction to Classification and
Number Building in Dewey, by Marty Bloomberg and Hans
Weber (Libraries Unlimited, 1976), and Dewey Decimal Classification: a study manual, 19th ed. by Jeanne Osborn (Libraries Unlimited, 1982). The third edition of Commonsense Cataloging, by Rosalind E. Miller and Jane C. Terwillegar (Bronx:
H. W. Wilson, 1983), has a helpful chapter called "Classifying
with Dewey."

Library of Congress Classification

The Library of Congress system is a widely used
general classification system that fills some thirty-odd volumes.
The notation is alphanumeric (i.e., includes both letters and
numbers) and irregular: some classes use single letters (E,
F), some two (HX, LB), some three (KFC). Finer breakdowns
are numerical, some using integers (HX1, F700), some decimal
fractions (KFC30.5, LB1028.5).

The Library of Congress system is uneven in its treatment of subjects, often inconsistent, and its notation is not
hierarchical in structure. Although it offers more separate
main classes than the Dewey system, it is harder to use because it lacks a comprehensive index. Consequently, even

catalogers in large and prestigious libraries find it difficult
to be consistent. Consider these two books for example:
Composition of Scientific Words, by R. W. Brown, and The
Scientist's Thesaurus, by G. F. Steffanides. Both serve
the same purposes and are almost identical in layout. Yet in
spite of these obvious similarities the Library of Congress
placed the one in class PE1175, the other in class Q179.

Other Classifications

Many special classification schemes have been published.
The National Library of Medicine, for example, has developed
a well-known system for medical books. Harvard University
has developed a classification for business literature. The
American Mathematical Society has published a classification
scheme for the field of mathematics. The Art Libraries Society of North America has published an art classification.
Volunteers or appointees in charge of small special libraries
will probably do best to adopt one of the published classification schemes designed for their type of library. Help and advice can be had from the Cataloging and Classification Section
of the Resources and Technical Services Division of the American Library Association, 50 East Huron Street, Chicago, IL
60611.

Help can also be had from the Special Libraries Association, 1700 Eighteenth Street, N.W., Washington, DC 20009.
The addresses of numerous other American and Canadian
library associations can be found in a useful directory entitled
Bowker Annual of Library and Book Trade Information, available from the R. R. Bowker Co., 205 East 42nd St. New
York, NY   10017

Form Classification

Subject arrangement is not the only alternative for the
organization of library materials. Some types of books are
best grouped on the shelves by their form rather than by
their subject. A collection of stories about railways, for example, might stand with other collections of the genre "stories," not with other books about railways. The plays of
Shakespeare, although they might deal with English history,
do not stand with other books about English history. Nor do

they stand with books about English literature. They <u>are</u>
English literature and stand with all other books by Shakespeare.

Often subject and form principles are combined. A
publication may be classed first by subject (for example,
political science) and then by form (for example, periodical).
The effect will be to separate political science materials that
are periodicals from those that are not periodicals.

In some classes a book may be arranged first by language, then by genre, followed by time period, and finally
subarranged by author. In such a classification books of like
genre stand together, such as all German poetry. But it is
also possible to group the books first by time period, then by
author, and last by genre. Now all books by an author stand
together, regardless of genre, perhaps all the plays, poems,
essays, and stories by Bertolt Brecht. Many other variations
are possible, all of which helps to explain why classification
is a difficult art.

CONSTRUCTING YOUR OWN
CLASSIFICATION SYSTEM

Should it be necessary to construct an original classification scheme--not recommended but unavoidable under
certain pressures of real life--the following guidelines are offered.

1.   There should be a separate class for every subject
field in which 25 to 50 books can be expected to fall. A
small library (under 5,000 volumes) should not need more
than 200 subject classes.

2.   The classes should be mutually exclusive, if possible.
These two classes are mutually exclusive: dogs, cats. They
are mutually exclusive in the sense that a cat cannot also be
a dog. The following two classes are not mutually exclusive:
dogs, poodles. They are not mutually exclusive because a
poodle is also a dog. It may be necessary in some cases
to have a hierarchical class structure showing genus-species
relationships. Ideally this should be handled by a class/
subclass structure, e.g. Class DOGS, Subclass 1 POODLES,
Subclass 2 TERRIERS, etc.

3. In addition to subject classes there should be a number of form classes, so called because they are places where books can be grouped together that share a certain format rather than a subject. Here are some suggested form classes:

> Atlases (collections of geographical maps)
> Bibliographies (lists of books, periodical indexes)
> Biographical directories (e.g. Who's Who)
> Dictionaries (books that define terminology)
> Directories (lists of firms, suppliers)
> Encyclopedias and handbooks
> Tables of numerical values

4. There should be a general or miscellaneous class. Any book that does not fit into one of the established form classes will be placed into its subject class. If it does not fit in any subject class either, it will go into the general class until a better place for it is found. Accumulations in the general or miscellaneous class will soon show what additional classes are needed in the system.

5. Short notations, no more than three or four symbols per line, should be adopted.

Step-by-Step Guide to Classifying

The work of classifying a book is in several steps. I suggest that the reader go over the following questions once or twice, then apply the steps to individual books that come up for classifying.

• Step 1. Is it a book about something (about the weather, for example, or about George Washington), or is it a book of a certain kind (a novel, for example, or a Spanish-English dictionary)?

• Step 2. If it is a book about something, is the entire book about the same thing or does it deal with several subjects?

• Step 3. If it deals with one subject, name that subject. Match that name with the narrowest of the established classes that will fit and assign the corresponding notation to the book.

• Step 4. If it deals with several subjects, can these
subjects all be said to be sub-topics of one broader topic?
If so, name the broader topic and match that name with the
best-fitting of the established classes. Assign the corresponding notation to the book.

• Step 5. If it deals with several subjects that cannot
be said to be sub-topics of one broader topic, name the topic
that is either most thoroughly covered or of predominant
interest to the type of user for whom the library exists.
Match that name with the best-fitting of the established classes. Assign the corresponding notation to the book.

• Step 6. If it is not a book about something so much
as a book of a certain format, name that format (dictionary?
encyclopedia? almanac? handbook? collection of tables? biblio-
graphy?) and match that name with the best-fitting of the established classes. Assign the corresponding notation to the
book.

• Step 7. If it is not a book about something so much
as a book containing a work or works of a certain genre, name
that genre (novel? poems? plays? children's fairy tales?).
Match that name with the best-fitting of the established classes. Assign the corresponding notation to the book.

Bibliographic listings such as the American Book Publishing Record regularly include Dewey and Library of Congress
class numbers for new books. This often helps classifiers
check on their own work and refine their understanding of
the system and the classifying process. However, just because someone else assigned a book to a certain class does
not guarantee that the result represents the best decision for
your library.

In a recent issue of the American Book Publishing
Record, for example, two books about survey sampling were
listed. One had been classed in Library of Congress QA276.6,
the other in HA31.2, which shows again that it is not simple
to keep like things together in a library. To decide what
constitutes "like things" remains a highly subjective business.

Chapter 3

LOCATION CODES OR
"CALL NUMBERS" _____

Books and other types of items are often kept in order on
their shelves by means of symbols that together constitute a
location code. Many librarians, remembering the days when
such codes were simple numbers and one had to call for one's
books at a counter after looking them up in the catalog, still
refer to the location code or parts of it as the "call number."

A location code or call number may consist of as many
as four parts:

    1.   File designation
    2.   Class symbol
    3.   Book symbol
    4.   Copy symbol

FILE DESIGNATIONS

The person who returns publications to their positions
in the file must be able to tell, of course, into which file they
belong. This is easy to do in the case of some kinds of publications. Current periodical issues, for example, are clearly
recognizable as such by their format and name. A book (in
the traditional sense) is identified by its shape and size as
a publication that belongs in the book stacks. Such publications do not need a special file designation. It is obvious in
which file they belong. But for a current periodical issue
to be distinguishable from a back issue, for example, or an
ordinary book from one relegated to the reference file, the
publications must carry visible file designations.

Designations for special files are arbitrary symbols, of course. The designation for certain reference books may be REF. Recordings may be housed in a file designated AUDIO, and so on. All file designations have two purposes in common: they serve to tell library personnel into which file any given publication needs to be put, and they tell the catalog user in which file a given publication can be found.

In most libraries the bulk of the books belongs to one general collection often referred to as "the stacks." This file needs no designation. The file designation for such a book, we might say, is implied. In other words, if the location code mentions no other file, and if the publication is not clearly placed into a special file due to its format (e.g. an audio-cassette), the book belongs in the stacks. Here is an example of a location code with an implied file designation:

811.52
B7
W5

Absence of a special file designation in this location code means that the book belongs in the general file, "the stacks." This particular location code, by the way, was assigned to a book entitled What the Woman Lived: Selected Letters of Louise Brogan. By contrast, here is the location code for a book entitled Historical Atlas of California. It resides in a specially designed piece of furniture called an atlas case, and it carries a special file designation:

ATLAS
CASE
911.784
B4

The file designation here is ATLAS CASE.

CLASS SYMBOLS

The second part of the location code is the class symbol. If the decimal classification is used, the class symbol for a certain book of short stories may be

813.54

If the Library of Congress system is used, the symbol may
be

     PZ4

or possibly

     PS 3562 .E42

     Some class symbols in the Dewey system are very long.
A certain book on the history of mountaineering, for example,
was given this number:

     796.52094947

Even bigger numbers are possible. Class symbols in the
Library of Congress system, too, can get unwieldy. A book
on nursing in the State of Oaxaca, Mexico, for example, might
carry this class symbol:

     RT
     7
     M6
     O2

Here RT 7 stands for nursing, M6 stands for Mexico, and O2
stands for Oaxaca. All of that is one class symbol. If the
library has several books on this topic, they all have the same
class symbol. To distinguish them from one another, book
symbols must be added to the location code.

<h2 style="text-align:center">BOOK SYMBOLS</h2>

     File designations and class symbols alone do not contain
all the information needed for a book to be found or replaced
on the shelf. Suppose you were using the classification system of the National Library of Medicine and you had placed
three books on hygiene in class QT275. There is nothing
in that class number that would place these three books on
the shelf in any particular relationship to each other. The
three books could stand like the illustration shown on the
next page or in some other order. They are not uniquely
identified, and in many libraries such lack of precision is not
desirable. Ideally, every book should have its definite place

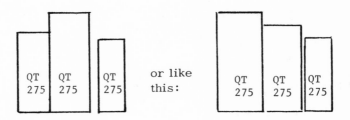

on the shelf. This is why libraries often add book symbols
to class symbols in order to compose a location code that is
unique. The book symbol, as its name indicates, identifies
the particular book. It is a symbol derived either from the
title or from the author's name.

Suppose the three books on hygiene, referred to above,
were entitled Modern Health, You and Your Body, and How to
Take Care of Yourself, respectively. Their location codes,
consisting of class symbol and book symbol, might be as
follows:

		QT	QT	QT
class symbol	{	275	275	275
book symbol		H7	M7	Y7

The book symbols H7, M7, and Y7 are merely short notations
for the first words in the titles, in alphabetical order:

    How   H7
    Modern M7
    You   Y7

There are several ways to construct book symbols. Some
libraries rely on the so-called Cutter Tables, a published
system of fixed symbols assigned to certain letter combinations
such as

             .

             .

    Bilby B 491
    Bile   B 492
    Bill   B 493

The Cutter system has the virtue of consistency. It
generates definite symbols for each combination of letters.
The other side of that coin, of course, is a certain lack of

flexibility. If a book entitled <u>Bill Before the House</u> carries
the book symbols B 493, a later acquisition in the same class
entitled <u>Bill Before Law</u> must be given an arbitrary number
interpolated between Bile and Bill, perhaps B 4925.

    A slightly more flexible system is the author number
system pioneered by the Library of Congress. Here, specific
letter combinations do not have fixed numbers. Instead, book
symbols are constructed afresh in each subject class according
to tables such as the one shown here:

   .
   .

2. After other initial consonants
     for second letter: a e i o r u
       use number: 3 4 5 6 7 8

Under this system, <u>Bill Before the House</u> in class A might
be assigned the symbols B5. <u>Bill Before Law</u>, if in another
class such as B, might get the same symbols, B5. But if
both books were in class A, then the second book might get
the symbol B4. Or if B4 had already been used, B45, or
some other number interpolated to preserve the alphabetical
order. The complete system of book numbers, actually designated "author" numbers by the Library of Congress, was
first published on pages 7 and 8 of the <u>Cataloging Service</u>
<u>Bulletin</u>, Number 107 for December 1973, published by the
Processing Department of the Library of Congress. The
system is also explained in <u>Introduction to Cataloging and</u>
<u>Classification</u>, by Bohdan Wynar (4th ed., 1972)

    Book numbers preserve alphabetical order, incidentally,
because they are treated as decimals. Thus the sequence B4,
B45, B4952, B5 is treated as if the numbers were written

      B 0.4   B 0.45   B 0.4952   B 0.5

This stratagem applies to Cutter numbers as well as to Library
of Congress author numbers.

    Some small libraries assign abbreviated book symbols.
A book on cancer entitled <u>Treatment of Cancer</u> and one entitled
<u>Treatment of Carcinoma</u> might both have the same location
code:

616.9   616.9
T   T

This diminishes the effectiveness of the location code. If
both are on the shelf a reader must now investigate which of
the two books he wants. If only one is on the shelf the
reader may inadvertently take home the wrong book. It is
better to establish unique book symbols based on a difference
in the wording of the titles so that different books are clearly
distinguishable:

616.9   616.9
T6   T7

...cancer   ...carcinoma

Similar advice applies to books that differ in terms of their
editions. The 6th edition (1966) of a certain book may bear
the location code

R
121
K5

The library now acquires the 7th edition (1983) of the same
book. The two editions rest side by side on the shelf. The
year of the later edition can be added to its location code
so that the books are clearly distinguished:

R
121
K5
1983

Since the book symbols as recommended here are based
on the title of the book, it will happen that books by a given
author are widely dispersed within a class. If it is desirable
to keep books in a class together by their authors, as for
example in a collection of literature, and the classification
system used does not collect them in one place, the book
symbol can be constructed on the basis of the author's name.
This, of course, is why the book symbols of the Library of
Congress are referred to as "author" numbers.

One idea behind author numbers is "collocation," a

technical term that means that all of an author's works in a
class stand in one place. It should be pointed out that collocation by means of author numbers is an illusion. It cannot
be done reliably. If all the works of an author were free
standing, separately cataloged units written by that author
alone, collocation would indeed be possible. But many works
are cooperative efforts of several authors, and many more are
embedded with other authors' works in collections. Book
numbers for such publications will have to be based on other
criteria, such as title, and this spoils the idea of collocation.
Nevertheless, here are the book numbers for the hygiene
books discussed on page 28. We assume that their authors'
names had been Able, Baker, and Chomsky, respectively:

QT	QT	QT
275	275	275
A2	B2	C5

Here is another example. Two stand-alone works by George
Robert Gissing, Nether World and Thyrza, are classed in
Dewey 823.8. The location codes may look as follows:

823.8	823.8
G45	G45
N3	T5

The book symbols here have been expanded and consist of
an author component (G45) and a title component (N3 and T5,
respectively).

Other expansions of the book symbol are possible. If
Nether World were also available in a Spanish translation by
Moreno, it might bear this location code:

823.8	Class
G45	Author
N3	Title
M7	Translator

Here is another possible treatment of the same book:

823.8
G15
N3m

where the "m" stands for the translator's name. Here is
still another possibility:

      823.8   Class
      G15   Author
      N3   Title
      Sp   Language

When a corporate agency can be considered to be the
author of the work or works in the item cataloged, the name
of that agency can be used to form the book number. In
this way all the law codes in a corporate library, for example,
could be made to stand together by state, as in this example:

    348   348   348
    C2   C2 ... T3
    M7   P3   H2

where C2 stands for California, T3 for Texas.

When two or more copies of the same book are in the
collection, a copy symbol is often added to the location code,
beginning with copy 2. Suppose a book designated by the
location code QT275 A2 is very popular and you have a total
of three copies in the library. They might be labelled as
follows:

    QT   QT   QT
    275   275   275
    A2   A2   A2
          c.2   c.3

The location code appears on the spine of the book and,
if pockets and cards are used for lending, on the pocket and
book card. Some libraries repeat the entire location code some-
where inside the book in case the label should fall off.

There was a time when location codes were hand-lettered
onto spines in white or black ink. Nowadays most libraries
type the code onto labels that are glued to spines, pockets,
and cards. To prevent spine labels from peeling off, many
libraries reinforce them with transparent tape that can be
bought for the purpose from library supply houses. Others
simply coat them generously with transparent glue before
shelving the books.

SUMMARY OF STEPS FOR
LOCATION CODES

1. Does the publication require a location code? Not all publications require them. Magazines, for example, often are kept on the shelves in alphabetical order by title.

2. If the publication does require a location code, does the publication belong to a special file that needs to be singled out? If so, assign a file designation.

3. Does the publication belong to a file that is arranged by accession numbers? If so, add the accession number to the file designation.

4. Does the publication belong to a classified file? Classify and assign the class symbol (notation).

5. Assign the book symbol from the title. Or, if the contents are all by one author, you may base the book symbol on the author's name.

6. Is this a second or subsequent copy of the same publication for this library? If so, add copy symbol to location code, but only on label and pocket and book card, not on the catalog cards.

PART II:

CATALOGING

Chapter 4

DESCRIPTION PRINCIPLE   _____

It is not enough to place publications onto the shelves of a
library. To retrieve the information contained in them a
catalog must be provided, an index to the library's collection
that will enable the reader to look up a clue such as an
author's name, a title, or a topic, and determine if the library
has the book or books sought, and if so, where they are
located. The books, in other words, have to be cataloged.

Essentially, cataloging is the art of describing and indexing bibliographic items that contain recorded information.
An item is described by writing down or otherwise recording
its title, its author(s) or editor(s), its publisher, place and
date of publication, and similar descriptive information, all
of which will be discussed in the following chapters.

An item is then indexed by the addition of headings to
item descriptions, headings that point to important characteristics such as authors' names, subjects, forms, and titles.

Before a publication can be described, however, the
cataloger must decide under what principle to describe it.
Two different description principles must be considered: the
document description principle and the set description principle. Under the document description principle, one physical
volume, one document, is described as an individual bibliographic entity. Under the set description principle, a larger
set of two or more documents is what is described in the
catalog record.

When a publication is a single document this decision

is easy: the document description principle applies.   But when
a publication consists of more than one document per item, a
choice may have to be made: the set as a whole may have a
title and the publication could be described as a set (set description principle is applied); or each book in the set may have
its own title, and the set could then be split up and its component books cataloged as separate units (document description
principle is applied).   Whether such a set will be split up in
a given library is a question of policy based on utility.

DOCUMENT DESCRIPTION PRINCIPLE

Here are some examples of the document description
principle in action.   The book shown at the top of page 7
is a book of type 1:

> Urinary Analysis and Diagnosis, 5th edition, by Louis
> Heinzelmann

It is described under the document description principle in
terms of the book title and author.   The phonograph record
shown on page 7 is another item of type 1:

> Symphony No.2 in D, by Johannes Brahms

It is also described under the document description principle
in terms of the disc title and author (composer).

The book shown on page 8 is an item of type 2:

> Concepts of Disease, edited by Joel G. Brunson

It, too, is described under the document description principle
in terms of the book title and author (or, in this case,
editor; in a bibliographic sense editorship is a form of authorship).

SET DESCRIPTION PRINCIPLE

Here are some examples of the set description principle.
The item shown in the lower part of page 8 is a set of type
7:

Advances in Librarianship, edited by Melvin J. Voigt

Since the individual volumes have no titles of their own, the
set must stay together. It is described under the set description principle in terms of the set title and editor.

The books shown at the top of page 9 are a set of type
8:

Climatology, by Arnold Becker and Joe Doe

These two books, together constituting one work, must also
stay together. They, too, are cataloged under the set description principle in terms of set title and set authors. The
two examples just shown required no decision. There was only
one possible way to describe and index them. But sometimes
there is a choice.

DECISION: DOCUMENT OR SET?

The set shown on page 9 is an example of an item that
requires a decision:

The Sixties: Radical Change in American Religion,
ed. by James M. Gustafson. Vol. 387 of the Annals
of the American Academy of Political and Social Science,
January 1970.

This is a set of type 6. If each volume of the set stands in
a different place (which would be quite logical since every
numbered volume in this set deals with a different topic), each
is cataloged as a single item under the document description
principle (one set of catalog cards for each volume). If such
a set is more useful standing together, however, it is cataloged as one item under the set description principle (just
one set of catalog cards for the entire set of books). The
following list of options may help catalogers to decide which
description principle to apply.

1. If the item cataloged is of types 1 or 2 (see chart
on page 6), the document description principle applies
without exception.

2.   If the item cataloged is of types 5, 7, or 8 (see
chart on page 6), the set description principle applies
without exception.

3.   If the item to be cataloged is of types 3, 4, or 6
(see chart on page 6), it is usually kept together,
i.e. the set description principle is applied. But the
set can also be taken apart and treated as so many
separate books, i.e. the document description principle
can be applied if a purpose is served thereby.   In
either case it may be necessary to make some relational
entries, a procedure that is discussed in chapter 10.

Chapter 5

THE MAIN ENTRY _____

Once the description principle for the publication to be cataloged has been decided upon, the actual cataloging can begin.
It is now time to construct the basic catalog record, the so-
called main entry.

By the term "entry" we mean one catalog record. For
the great majority of items it is correct to say that an entry
is the same thing as a catalog card. But sometimes the catalog
record is so extended (long title, several authors, etc.) that
it takes two or more cards to hold all the information. In
such a case the entry comprises the entire decklet of cards.

It should be noted that not all librarians agree with this
terminology. Some use the term "entry" to designate the
heading that appears across the top of a card. In this book
the term "entry" always means "one catalog record." For
emphasis, we will sometimes use the somewhat redundant term
"entry record" to make sure readers understand that what is
meant is a record, not a heading.

By "main entry" we mean that entry which constitutes
the complete catalog record of the item. In the ALA Glossary
a main entry is defined as the "complete catalog record of a
bibliographic item."

For each item cataloged we must make a main entry.
If needed we can make added entries. An added entry record,
like a main entry record, is also a catalog record of a bibliographic item. But it is not necessarily as complete as the
main entry record, and in addition it carries an added entry

heading across the top. These headings give access by
authors' names, subjects, forms, or titles, as needed. A discussion of added entry records and their headings begins with
chapter 7. In chapters 5 and 6 we are concerned only with
the main entry.

What information is needed for a complete catalog record?
And how shall this information be arranged on the catalog
card? Opinions are divided. Some librarians distinguish between author main entries (complete catalog records that carry
the name of one author as a heading at the top), uniform title
main entries (complete catalog records that carry a uniform
title as a heading at the top), and plain title main entries
(complete catalog records that have no headings but begin
with the title). A distinction is also made between closed
entries and open entries. Each type of main entry is constructed to slightly different specifications spelled out in a
code that is followed widely, the <u>Anglo-American Cataloguing</u>
<u>Rules</u> (AACR2).

To decide which type of main entry to make from case
to case requires mastery of chapter 21 of AACR2, a 70-page
treatise so complex that even the highly trained and skilled
librarians at the Library of Congress are not always consistent
in their application of the rules of entry. Obviously, in
small libraries personnel specially trained to cope with such
esoteric knowledge is seldom available. This is why, rather
than allow the cataloging operation to bog down in a maze of
seemingly unmanageable complications, I propose a simplification
of this process. For small libraries I recommend that all main
entries be constructed as title main entries. By this stratagem
one rule will apply to all publications. No exceptions.

A title main entry record consists of five elements of
bibliographic information:

1. The bibliographic description of the item, beginning
with the title of the item

2. The physical description of the item (optional)

3. Notes (optional)

4. Tracings, a record of all added entries made

5. Location code, sometimes designated the "call number"

Just what data make up these elements will be explained in chapter 6. Here we are concerned only with the general form of the main entry record.

TITLE MAIN ENTRY LAYOUT

Here is a printed Library of Congress card, a title main entry record produced according to AACR2:

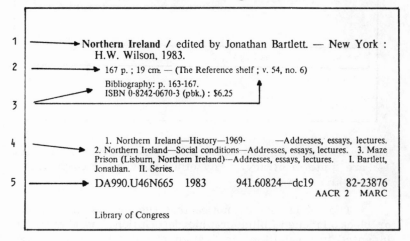

1   → **Northern Ireland /** edited by Jonathan Bartlett. — New York : H.W. Wilson, 1983.

2   → 167 p. ; 19 cm. — (The Reference shelf ; v. 54, no. 6)

      Bibliography: p. 163-167.
      ISBN 0-8242-0670-3 (pbk.) : $6.25

3

4   1. Northern Ireland—History—1969-   —Addresses, essays, lectures. 2. Northern Ireland—Social conditions—Addresses, essays, lectures.   3. Maze Prison (Lisburn, Northern Ireland)—Addresses, essays, lectures.   I. Bartlett, Jonathan. II. Series.

5   → DA990.U46N665   1983   941.60824—dc19   82-23876
      AACR 2   MARC

Library of Congress

Legend: 1. Bibliographic description; 2. Physical description; 3. Notes; 4. Tracings; 5. Call number.

The five elements are labelled. (1) is the bibliographic description, done in the format known as the International Standard Bibliographic Description (ISBD); (2) points to the physical description, sometimes called "collation," which is optional; (3) points to the notes, also optional; (4) shows the tracings; and (5) includes two styles of call numbers, Library of Congress and Dewey.

When cards are typed locally the layout can be simplified, but it is best to follow one set of typographic specifica-

tions throughout so that all cards have the same indentions.
One possible card layout is illustrated below.

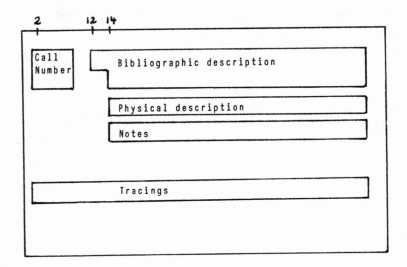

The indentions, or spaced margins, shown here--2, 12, and
14--are quite arbitrary.   Any other convenient combination
will do just as well.

      The reader should notice that the topmost paragraph
or block, labelled "bibliographic description," is always typed
indented to the left, or in "hanging" indention.   It always
contains the bibliographic description which, as we shall see
in Chapter 6, always begins with the title of the item cataloged.
The effect of the indention is that the title always stands out
on the card.   And since such a main entry record begins with
the title of the item, it is referred to as a "title main entry."

On page 45 is the picture of another complete title main entry
record.

```
BF
441        Identifying and solving problems : a
K27          system approach / Roger Kaufman. --
             La Jolla, CA : University Associates,
             1976.
             iv, 121 p. : ill. ; 16 x 23 cm.




1. PROBLEM SOLVING.  I. Kaufman, Roger A.
```

The reader will have noticed that in all examples the location code or "call number" occupies a special block in the upper left hand corner of the card. When word processing is employed, it may be slightly inconvenient or inefficient to program for a separate block in that position. It may be easier to print cards line by line. In such cases the location code can be given as a note, as in this example:

```
                Larousse encyclopedia of European
                  history / General editor: Joseph
                  Hyslop. -- New York : Klamm, 1945.
                  508 p.

                LOCATION: 909 L2




1. EUROPE--HISTORY.  I. Hyslop, Joseph, ed.
```

All our sample cards, however, will show the location code
in the traditional upper left corner.

    Sometimes there is more cataloging information than
fits on the front of one card. In such cases one can continue
to type on the back of the card (upside down and hole at the
top for easier reading when the card is held in the tray by
the rod) or one can make one or more extension cards for the
entry. Here is an example of an entry that consists of a card
and an extension card:

```
F              History of Los Angeles County,
868               California, with illustrations,
L8                descriptions of its scenery,
R7                residences, fine blocks and
                  manufactories, from original
                  sketches by artists of the
                  highest ability / edited by
                  William Willoughby Robinson
                  and Clara Pintel Diamond.
                  Berkeley, CA : Howell, 1948.
   (continued on next card)
```

```
F              History of Los Angeles County,
868                               card 2 of 2
L8
R7                192 p.
                  Reproduction of the Thompson
                  edition of 1885.




   1. LOS ANGELES (COUNTY), CALIFORNIA.
   I. Robinson, William Willoughby, ed.
```

OTHER TYPES OF MAIN ENTRIES

Most catalog entries made according to the instructions
of AACR2 are author main entry records, incorporating an
author main entry heading above the bibliographic description.
The idea of constructing a main entry record with an author
heading on top derives from the correct observation that
many items are stand-alone works by one author or collections
of several works all by one author. In such cases it is quite
logical to consider the author's name the most important element of the bibliographic description and to construct a main
entry record in such a way that the author's name in filing
order (inverted, last name first) stands at the head, above
the title.

Here is another example. It begins with the name of the
author in a separate paragraph or heading at the top of the
card. Note that the entire card is the main entry, or main
entry record. The line at the top, "Kaufman, Roger A.," is
the main entry heading. The paragraph below the heading,
beginning with the word "Identifying" and ending with "1976,"
is the bibliographic description, complete with author's name
in regular form, first name first.

```
BF        Kaufman, Roger A.
441           Identifying and solving problems : a
K27       system approach / Roger Kaufman. -- La
          Jolla, CA : University Associates, 1976.
             iv, 121 p. : ill. ; 16 x 23 cm.




          1. PROBLEM SOLVING. I. Title.
```

Many items are issued under the sponsorship of a corporate agency rather than by an author in the usual sense.
Under certain circumstances this calls for a so-called cor-

porate author main entry, a main entry record that carries the
name of a corporate body as a heading above the bibliographic
description. Here is an example:

Main entry

```
                                                                    Main
                                                                    entry
                                                                    heading
    Texas Instruments Incorporated.   Learning Center.
        Understanding calculator math : getting together the basic ⎤  Biblio-
    information, formulas, facts, and mathematical tools you need to │  graphic
    "unlock" the real power of your handheld calculator at home, on  ⎬  descrip-
    the job, in school or college, throughout your everyday life /   │  tion
    ₍developed by Texas Instruments Learning Center₎. -- Dallas :     ⎦
    The Center, c1978.
        224 p. in various pagings : ill. ; 21 cm.  -- (Understanding series)
        Bibliography: p.. B1-B3.
        Includes index.
        ISBN 0-89512-016-X

        1. Calculating-machines—Problems, exercises, etc.   I. Title.   II. Series.
    QA75.T38   1978                         510'.28'5                   78-50808
                                                                        MARC

        Library of Congress                 78
```

    Unfortunately, the principle of making a main entry
under an author heading is often very difficult to carry out
because determining authorship is by no means always a
simple matter. While all works, of course, have been written
or created by persons, or authors, the names of these persons
are not always known. Some items contain many works by
different authors and no one author can be said to be responsible for the entire item. In cases where the author cannot
be determined, a title main entry is called for, according to
AACR2.

    A regular or "natural" title main entry, AACR2 style,
was shown on page 43. That example was a closed title main
entry, i.e., a main entry for a book that was complete when
published. Note that the date followed the publisher's name.

    An open title main entry is shown on page 49. This is
a main entry for a regularly published series, a book that keeps
being issued year after year in separate volumes. Note that
by AACR2 specifications the date in this case precedes the
publisher's name.

Main entry

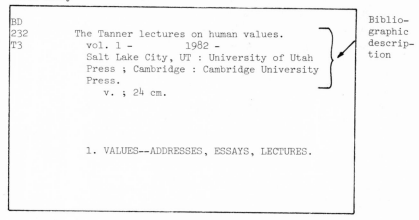

```
BD                                                            Biblio-
232      The Tanner lectures on human values.         ⎫      graphic
T3           vol. 1 -          1982 -                 ⎪      descrip-
             Salt Lake City, UT : University of Utah  ⎬ ←   tion
             Press ; Cambridge : Cambridge University ⎪
             Press.                                   ⎭
               v. ; 24 cm.
```

```
          1. VALUES--ADDRESSES, ESSAYS, LECTURES.
```

Some publications are best kept together under an arti-
ficial collective title, a so-called uniform title. A typical uniform title main entry looks like this:

Main entry

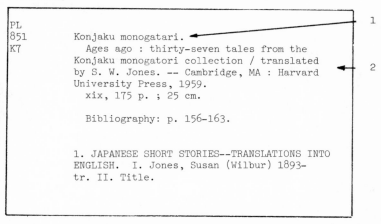

```
PL                                                        ←──── 1
851      Konjaku monogatari. ←
K7           Ages ago : thirty-seven tales from the
         Konjaku monogatori collection / translated
         by S. W. Jones. -- Cambridge, MA : Harvard  ←── 2
         University Press, 1959.
             xix, 175 p. ; 25 cm.

         Bibliography: p. 156-163.


         1. JAPANESE SHORT STORIES--TRANSLATIONS INTO
         ENGLISH.  I. Jones, Susan (Wilbur) 1893-
         tr. II. Title.
```

Legend: 1. Main entry heading, contains the title of the
collection from which the stories in this book are taken;
2. Bibliographic description, beginning with the actual
title of the item.

Uniform title main entries and author main entries are not
recommended in this book. For a discussion of how to build
a natural title main entry, however, the reader should now
turn to chapter 6.

Chapter 6

WHAT GOES ON THE TITLE MAIN ENTRY   _____

The previous chapter stated that the title main entry record consists of five elements: (1) the bibliographic description, (2) the physical description, (3) notes, (4) tracings, and (5) location code. These elements need to be discussed in detail.

THE BIBLIOGRAPHIC DESCRIPTION

The bibliographic description typically consists of the title, statement of authorship, edition statement, and imprint.

Title

This first element is always present in any bibliographic record. If the item does not have a title, the cataloger must give it one. There can be no exceptions because the title is the one element without which a publication cannot be described. A catalog card without a title would be an incomplete catalog record. As far as the bibliographic description is concerned, therefore, all publications have a title, a name given to them either by their creators or by some later bibliographer.

In the case of a book in the traditional sense, the title is taken from the title page. In other types of publications the title is taken from the equivalent of the title page such as the masthead of a periodical, the label of a phonograph record, the title frame of a filmstrip, or such. (Note: do not use the title on the spine of a book or the colorful but often inaccurate jacket of a cassette or record!)

It is not always easy to say just which words on a title page comprise the title of the book in hand. A book called Go in Beauty has a simple title. There is nothing more to say. But what if the title page reads Hoyt's Basic Business Methods? Is "Hoyt's" part of the title? Or is the title Basic Business Methods? A simple rule of thumb is to record the fullest form of the title. If it is likely that library users might look under the other part of the title, an added entry can be made. More about title added entries in chapter 8.

If a publication contains two or three works and has no overall title of its own, the librarian will simply string the titles together:

Going home ; Man in the mirror ; Dust and duty /

The punctuation between titles (space, semicolon, space) is that of the International Standard Bibliographic Description (ISBD).

If the publication contains many works, however, this is not practical. Some publishers will pick the title of one of the works and add a descriptive phrase to make a title for the item:

Horseflesh, and other stories

The librarian can adopt the same strategy to make up titles for collections of any kind that have no firm item titles. Here is the title of a disc recording structured that way:

Carnaval, op. 9 [and other music]

The parenthetical statement indicates that other bands on the recording contain different compositions. The brackets (or parentheses, if the typewriter or word processor at hand does not have brackets) indicate that that portion of the title was supplied by the librarian.

Some publications have very long titles. It is sometimes expedient to record a shortened title in such cases, ending with ellipses. Never, however, should one shorten the beginning of a title. It causes filing and finding problems.

Occasionally a publication contains a work that is known

by two titles. An example is Beethoven's Sonata in C# minor,
op. 27, no. 2., which is also known as Moonlight Sonata. In
a scholarly library the official title may be preferred. The
bibliographic description then begins with the word "Sonata."
The popular title "Moonlight Sonata" can be accessed through a
title added entry. In some other type of library it may be
better to use the popular title. The word "Moonlight" then
leads the bibliographic description, and the official title is
relegated to a note.

It is good library practice to record all titles verbatim,
word-for-word as shown on the title page. One departure
can be recommended: drop the leading article in the nominative case. For speakers of English, where cases have lost
their meaning, this is an easy matter: if any English language
title begins with a, an, or the, those articles are dropped.
If the title of an item is The Future of Corrections, record it
as Future of Corrections. Since "The" is not a filing word,
this stratagem makes finding easier.

Leading articles in other languages are not always so
quickly detected. A person who does not know Spanish, for
example, will be hard put to distinguish between Los burros
(drop "Los," an article in the nominative case) and Los de
abajo (do not drop "Los," a pronoun). If, therefore, this
rule causes a problem the best policy will be to ignore all
English leading articles and to regard all others (and hope
that not too many non-English books will find their way into
the library).

Some titles of books begin with single letters. Here is
a mock title page to illustrate:

B.E.F.

The Whole Story

of the

Bonus Army

Such single letters must be recorded on the card precisely
as found on the title page, with periods separating them:
B.E.F.: the whole story of the Bonus Army. This signals
to the filer that B, E, and F are separate strings or words,
filed as such. Contrast that title with the one that follows:

ABC Algol

Since ABC is written without spaces, or as one string or word, it must be recorded on the card in that way: ABC Algol.

If a title begins with numerals, they must also be recorded on the card in this way.   Here is a mock title page:

19
Necromancers
from Now

Here is the corresponding title as recorded on the card:
19 necromancers from now.

If a title begins with a word that is not English but is written in Latin letters it is transcribed as found on the title page, without translation:

Dommage, my dear Ernie : a play.

If a non-English title is given in a non-Latin alphabet, however, it must be transliterated into Latin letters before it can be recorded (only transliterated, not translated):

becomes "Nihon gendai...." The cataloger who does not read Japanese must get help, as the author did in this case.

Author Statement

The term "author" includes composers, compilers, editors, translators, and other types of persons and agencies that can be said to be responsible for a publication.

The names of personal authors are given as they appear in the item. Thus, if the title page reads

A
SHORT HISTORY
OF THE
WORLD

H. G. Wells

the author's name in the bibliographic description is given
as H. G. Wells. If the author's name is preceded by the
word "by" or its equivalent in another language, those words
are included in the author statement. Thus, if the title page
reads

RED MEN AND WHITE

BY

OWEN WISTER

the author statement following the title in the bibliographic
description becomes "by Owen Wister."

Some author situations get very complicated. Consider
the following title page:

The Legacy of

GREECE

Essays by Gilbert Murray, W. R. Inge,
J. Burnet, Sir T. L. Heath, D'Arcy W.
Thompson, Charles Singer, R. W.
Livingstone, A. Toynbee, A. E. Zimmern,
Percy Gardner, Sir Reginald Blomfield

Edited by

R. W. Livingstone

The cataloger must first decide where the title ends and where
the author statement begins. According to the Anglo-American
Cataloguing Rules, 2nd ed. (AACR2), the title of this book
is "The Legacy of Greece: Essays." The first part, The
Legacy of Greece, is called the title proper. The second part,
Essays, is called other title information. This book has two
author statements. The first begins with "by Gilbert Murray"

and the second is "Edited by R. W. Livingstone." Since the
first group of authors consists of more than three names, the
author statement in the bibliographic description is shortened
to just the first name followed by ellipses and a parenthetic
Latin abbreviation indicating that there are others: "by Gilbert Murray... [et al.]". Some will prefer to anglicize and
make it "by Gilbert Murray [and others]". On the catalog
card the two author statements are separated by a semicolon.
More on punctuation can be found on page 61. More on the
form of authors' names is in chapter 8.

    Names of groups or agencies that are considered to be
serving as authors are also given in the bibliographic description as shown on the title page. Thus, if a title page
reads

COMPUTERS

by the

Editors of Scientific American

the author statement in the bibliographic description reads
"by the editors of Scientific American." If the title page
reads

WORKSHOP ON
SOLAR HEATING

Sponsored by

The National Science Foundation

the author statement reads "sponsored by the National Science
Foundation." More on corporate authors is in chapter 8.

    Whenever the information on the title page is unclear,
the cataloger may add necessary words in brackets. If this
were the title page,

BEOWULF

Jane Doe

it would be appropriate, since Jane Doe did not write this
Anglo-Saxon classic, to give the author statement as "[edited
by] Jane Doe."

Edition Statement.

  This data element is of course needed only for second
or subsequent editions of a publication. It is simplest to
give the edition in numerical form in a standard format,
i.e., 2nd ed., even if the title page states "Second edition."
If the title page states "Revised and greatly enlarged edition,"
it is sufficient to reduce the edition statement to "rev. ed."

  It should be noted that each separately numbered edition
of a book is cataloged as a separate item unless the cataloger
decides that a so-called open entry record would be more useful. In an open entry no finite date is given, only the date
the publication first started, followed by a hyphen, as in
1976- .

Imprint.

  Typically, this includes place of publication, name of
publisher or producer, and date of publication. The imprint
information is taken from the title page, front or back, or
comparable source of information if the item cataloged is not
a book.

  The date is usually found on the back of the title page
of a book, the verso. Very often more than one date appears.
The cataloger should use the latest copyright date. Thus,
a book may have been published in 1980, but inspection of
the back of the title page reveals that it is the third printing
and that the copyright date is 1972. This means that the
last time some new information was added to the book was
1972, and it is that date that should be shown in the record.

  Some librarians will want to be very technical about
this and specify a copyright date by a lowercase "c" prefixed
to the date: c1972. Some will even want to give both dates:
1980 (c1972). There is something to be said for simply
making it a policy to take the latest copyright date and state
it without "c," as in

   New York : Appels, 1972.

  Occasionally an old book that is in the nature of a
classic is reprinted. Frequently such a book carries a new

title page that makes it look like a brand new item. The imprint should be based on the new title page, but the fact that
it is a reprint of an older edition should be indicated in a
note:

Imprint = New York : Peters, 1982

Note = Reprint. Originally Boston : Gower, 1881

More about notes can be found below.

In multi-document items the various documents or volumes
sometimes have different publication dates. It is best, in such
cases, to give the range of dates from the earliest to the
latest:

Chicago : Jobes, 1968-1974

Publications that still continue to be published cannot,
of course, be given a definite date. Here is the imprint
for a typical magazine or periodical, the imprint for an "open
entry":

New York : American Heritage Publication Co., 1958-

The hyphen after the year indicates that this is the beginning
year of the publication and that it is still being published.
Even if the library does not have a complete run going back
to the beginning, the imprint date should always be the starting date of the publication. Holdings can be indicated by a
note:

Library has 1970-

Some publications are published at irregular intervals.
The library may have a policy of acquiring all editions of a
certain series as they appear but not wish to make separate
catalog entries for each new edition. Open entry is a good
stratagem here, too. Instead of cataloging each book separately as "Fodor's Budget Germany 80," "Fodor's Budget Germany
81," "Fodor's Budget Germany 82," and so on, it would be
better to create one record for Fodor's Budget Germany...
(using ellipses instead of the date that appears as part of
the title) and indicate the years held by a "Library has"
note such as the one following on page 59.

Library has latest edition only

If place of publication and date cannot be determined, as in the case of many nonbook items, the producer's name may be all that can be given in the imprint:

Granada Records.

Such nonbook materials often have unique label numbers that can be used for precise identification. Label numbers can be given in a note. More about that below under "Notes."

THE PHYSICAL DESCRIPTION

The physical description of the item, as opposed to the bibliographic description discussed above, gives the size and dimensions of the item, such as number of pages, number of volumes, length, height, diameter, running time, or other suitable measurement.

In small libraries the physical description, also referred to as the "collation," is often reduced to a minimum. Instead of

xiv, 450 p. : ill., maps ; 24cm.

a small library's catalog card may simply say:

450 p.

In other words, only the most essential information is given.

Here is the complete physical description for a three-volume set of books:

3 v. (1633 p.) : ill. ; 24cm.

Note that number of volumes and total number of pages are given. A small library may reduce this to

3 v.

For a periodical or other serial the final number of volumes cannot be stated. Here is a way to show that other volumes are to follow:

v. 1-

The beginning volume designation for a periodical is considered
in this book to be part of the physical description. Other au-
thorities add this information to the imprint, before the date.

Of course, it is possible to describe a publication without
giving any collation. But few libraries practice such austerity
since readers usually want to have an idea of the size of the
publication described.

For some types of publications a medium designation is
added to the physical description. If the cataloged item, for
example, contains a score or a part, in other words consists
primarily of musical symbols, printed on paper, the medium
designation "Music" leads the physical description. Materials
other than print on paper are also given suitable designations
such as "Microform," "Audiocassette," "Sound disc," etc.
If an audiovisual item consists of more than one unit this fact
can be combined with the medium designation: "2 audiotapes."
Here is the physical description or collation for a book consisting
mostly of printed music:

Music. 110 p.

Here is the physical description for a phonograph record:

1 sound disc : 33 1/3 rpm, stereo ; 12 in.

This includes medium, playing speed, recording mode, and
diameter, in that order. The punctuation is that of the International Standard Bibliographic Description (ISBD). A small
library might shorten this, without loss, to

Sound disc, 33 1/3

Since designating the medium of publication is a matter of physical description, this information leads the physical description
block. Other writers recommend that the medium information be
added to the title in the bibliographic description. By tradition,
no medium designation is given for books and periodicals.

NOTES

Any other helpful information not given in the bibliogra-

phic or physical description can be added as notes. Here are
some examples of notes:

> Annals of Mathematics, v.13 (a series note)

> Reprint of the 1879 ed.

> Liverpool Symphony, George Cox, Conductor (a per-
> former note)

> Contents: Beowulf.--Song of Roland.--Kalevala (a
> contents note)

> Library has latest edition only (a holdings note)

In small libraries bibliographic notes are used sparingly because
they are not absolutely necessary for the description of an item.
But they can be helpful to catalog users.

TRACINGS

This part of the bibliographic record lists all headings or
access points other than the title, which leads the bibliographic
description. These headings and their tracings will be further
discussed under "Added Entries" beginning with chapter 7.

LOCATION CODE OR "CALL NUMBER"

Chapter 3 deals with this topic.

PUNCTUATION

The various elements of the bibliographic description--
the title, author statement, edition statement, and so forth--
can be separated from each other by periods and commas as
common sense directs. But the punctuation system of the International Standard Bibliographic Description (ISBD) may be
employed to advantage because it standardizes punctuation.
The idea is to indicate by punctuation conventions where one
element ends and another begins, independent of language.
Thus, space-colon-space separates the title proper from other
title information, as in:

Dommage, my dear Ernie : a play

Space-slash-space separates the title from the author statement,
as in

...a play / by Joe Doe

Period-space-double hyphen-space separate the author from the
edition statement, as in

by Joe Doe. -- 3rd ed.

and so on. Here is a comprehensive example:

Great victory : the memoirs of a prince / by Fuji
Haramake; transl. by Tom Reid. -- 2nd ed. -- New
York : Appels, 1968.

All sample cards in this book are shown in ISBD form.

Here is another example of a complete main entry showing
all five elements:

Main entry

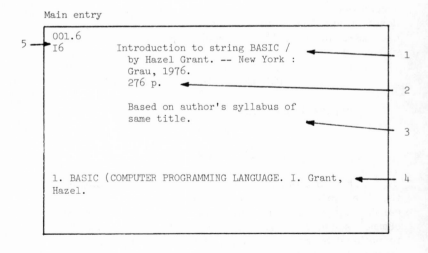

Legend: 1. Bibliographic description (title, author statement, and imprint); 2. Physical description; 3. Note;
4. Tracings; 5. Location code or Call number.

This main entry is for a "one-shot" book, an item that is complete in one volume.

Two other main entries that show all five parts of the description are pictured below. The first is for a book, an anthology. The second is for a floppy disk. Notice that the task of cataloging is essentially the same regardless of the medium of publication.

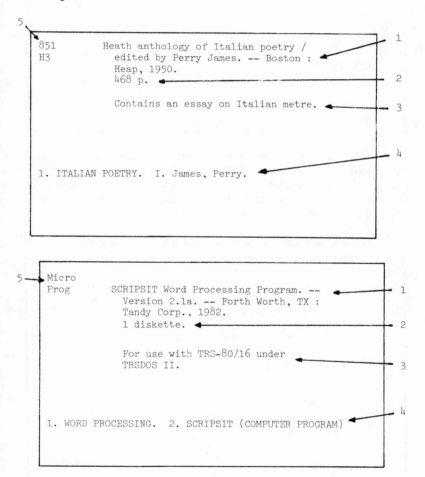

Here is another main entry, a so-called open entry:

```
FIN
A6          Almanach of investment information ... --
              New York : Buspress, 1965-

              Published every other year.
              Numbered on spine: 1-




1. INVESTMENTS.
```

The main entry above is made for sets that are not complete
but continue to appear periodically. No physical description is
given because it varies from issue to issue. The ellipses after
the title indicate that there was more information on the title
page, in this case "1965/66," "1967/68," and so on.

Here is a main entry that does not have any notes:

```
909
L2          Larousse encyclopedia of European history /
              General editor: Joseph Hyslop. -- New
              York : Klamm, 1945.
              508 p.




1. EUROPE--HISTORY.  I. Hyslop, Joseph, ed.
```

SUMMARY OF STEPS IN MAKING
A MAIN ENTRY RECORD

1. Decide which description principle is appropriate for the item.

2. Devise the location code and type it on the upper left corner of the card or as a note below the physical description.

3. Type bibliographic description, always beginning with the first word of the title that is not an article in the nominative case, in hanging indention format.

4. Directly below, or leaving a line free if space permits, type the physical description in a paragraph or block that is not indented. This block is sometimes referred to as the collation.

5. Below the physical description, type any necessary notes in paragraphs that are not indented.

6. After deciding what added entries are needed (see chapter 7 and further), type appropriate tracings across the bottom of the card. The result is a complete title main entry.

THE MARC FORMAT

With increasing frequency now, personnel working in libraries will hear and read about MARC tapes, the MARC format, and MARC tags. The acronym comes from the machine readable cataloging project of the Library of Congress. Under the auspices of that institution a large body of cataloging information has been recorded on magnetic tapes. This information is shared by many libraries worldwide. The bibliographic information stored on these tapes is arranged in a precise record format of fields and sub-fields so that the various elements of the catalog record can be reliably retrieved from the tapes and from automated catalogs based on them. Each field in the MARC format has a number or "tag." A subject heading, for example, would be stored in a field tagged 650. On page 66, for comparison, are the five elements of a main entry that were listed above, this time together with their corresponding MARC fields and subfields.

ELEMENT	MARC TAG	MARC NAME
1. Bibliographic description	Field 245	Title statement
	Subfield a	Title proper
	Subfield b	Subtitle
	Subfield c	Statement of responsibility (i.e. authorship)
	Field 250	Edition statement
	Field 260	Imprint
	Subfield a	Place of publication
	Subfield b	Name of publisher
	Subfield c	Date of publication
2. Physical description	Field 300	Physical description
3. Notes	Fields 400-490	Series statements
	Fields 500-590	Notes
4. Tracings	Fields 100-130	Main entry (the editors of MARC do not use ALA terminology. What these fields actually contain are the headings of author and uniform title main entry records)
	Field 240	Uniform title (i.e. not in a heading)
	Fields 600-653	Subject added entries (the editors of MARC do not use ALA terminology. What these fields actually contain are subject headings)
	Field 655	Genre heading
	Fields 700-740	Added entry (the editors of MARC do not use ALA terminology. What these fields actually contain are author and title added entry headings)
5. Location code	Field 050	LC Call number
	Field 082	Dewey Decimal Classification number

A note concerning terminology: To distinguish between titles found on title pages and titles supplied by librarians, I have called them natural titles and uniform titles, respectively. Other books will distinguish between titles, uniform titles, and supplied titles.

The word "title," furthermore, is sometimes used in the special sense of "title proper." The title proper is the first part of a title when a subtitle is present. Thus, if the entire title of a book is

Prison : True case histories

the word "Prison" is the title proper.

Chapter 7

ADDED ENTRIES _____

The title main entry record is filed, of course, under the first
word of the title as typed in the bibliographic description.
This is a satisfactory access point for the library user who is
looking for the publication in the catalog under that first word
of the title. The reader looking for the book Introduction to
String BASIC will find it by looking under the word "introduction." But how about the reader who is looking for the
book on BASIC by Grant, or the library patron who just needs
information on BASIC?

The answer is quite simple. The cataloger makes additional records, called added entries, that are filed under
different access points. To provide access by author or by
an alternate form of the title, author added entries and title
added entries are made. These are discussed in detail in
chapter 8. To provide access by subject or other categories,
subject added entries are made, discussed in chapter 9.

An added entry has the following format (see page 69).
The reader should notice that on added entries, as on the main
entry, only the bibliographic description paragraph is indented.
All other paragraphs are typed straight, without indentions.
The tracings are usually omitted on added entries when the cards
are individually typed.

Added entry

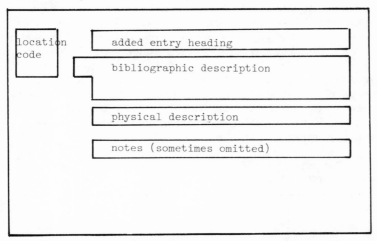

Such added entry records are essentially copies of the main entry record with different headings typed across the top. This practice is sometimes referred to as the unit card system of cataloging. The advantage for users is that they find complete information about the item no matter under what heading they may have found it.

Here is an example of a subject added entry based on a unit card. Note that the tracings and notes are omitted.

Added entry

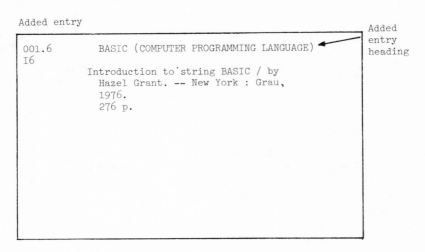

Added entry heading

In libraries where cards are typed individually (rather than run off automatically on a word processor or electronic typewriter, for example, or where printed cards are bought) the staff often skimps on the typing and does not repeat the complete unit card record on each added entry. To a point, such economy is reasonable. But it should stop at the bibliographic description. Even a shortened added entry should always repeat at least the bibliographic description exactly as given on the main entry. This preserves the unit card principle, essentially, which is a great help when it comes to catalog maintenance and library housekeeping.

Compare the added entry above with the shortened version that follows:

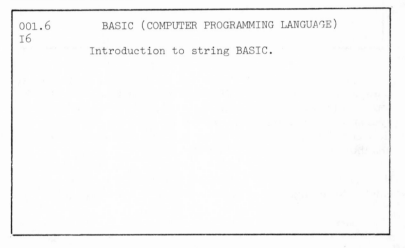

```
001.6          BASIC (COMPUTER PROGRAMMING LANGUAGE)
I6
                Introduction to string BASIC.
```

On such a card the user is given no clue as to whose introduction this is, what edition, how old, how big, etc. An unsatisfactory, frustrating sort of catalog!

A note concerning terminology: The term "added entry," according to the ALA Glossary, definition 2, designates any bibliographic record additional to the main entry record. This is the meaning of added entry throughout this book. Many librarians, however, distinguish between added entries and subject entries. If that narrower definition is accepted, the term added entry comprises only author and title added entries.

Chapter 8

AUTHOR AND TITLE ADDED ENTRIES _____

PERSONAL AUTHOR ENTRIES

Suppose a publication to be cataloged contains one work that
has one person named as author. An author added entry
must be made for this. Here is an example:

Added entry

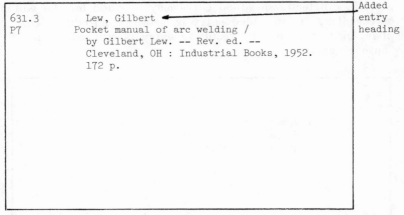

```
                                                        Added
631.3        Lew, Gilbert ◀━━━━━━━━━━━━━━━━━━━━        entry
P7           Pocket manual of arc welding /             heading
                by Gilbert Lew. -- Rev. ed. --
                Cleveland, OH : Industrial Books, 1952.
                172 p.
```

This author added entry is filed in the catalog under "Lew."

An author added entry is also made if the publication
contains many works by one author (see the example on page
72).

```
LIT            Doe, Joe
D7
               Six contemporary plays / by Joe
               Doe. -- New York : Holst, 1990.
```

If a publication contains many works by different
authors, those authors are not usually singled out by added
entries. Instead, an added entry may be made for the editor
or compiler. If an added entry is made for an editor, compiler, or translator, the resulting entry is still called an
"author" entry:

```
520.1          Gluck, Hanna
P7
               Progress in astronomy / edited by
               Hanna Gluck. -- London : Astronomical
               Society, 1988.
```

If two or more persons cooperated in writing the work
that is contained in a publication, then separate entry records

should be prepared for all authors. If the list of cooperating authors or editors gets too long (more than three, perhaps) most libraries refrain from making added entries for any but the first named. From a point of logic this makes no sense, but it is defensible on practical, economic grounds.

Non-Books

It is possible, even likely, that some of the publications cataloged in a small library are not books. They may be periodicals, pamphlets, or cassettes. For the cataloger, the distinction between books and non-books is of no consequence. A publication, any type of publication, is represented in the catalog by a title main entry. If the publication has a personal author in the extended bibliographic sense, a personal author added entry is made for that publication. Here is the author added entry for the composer of the music recorded on a phonograph record:

Personal Author Added Entry

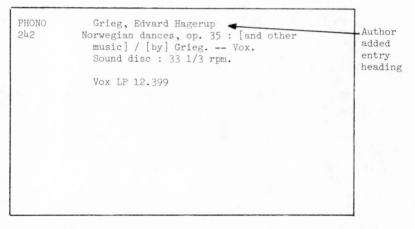

```
PHONO      Grieg, Edvard Hagerup  ◄──────        ──Author
242        Norwegian dances, op. 35 : [and other         added
           music] / [by] Grieg. -- Vox.                  entry
           Sound disc : 33 1/3 rpm.                      heading

           Vox LP 12.399
```

While the label on the record gives the composer's name simply as "Grieg," the cataloger must supply the full name in the catalog heading to prevent confusion between authors with identical surnames. Once the form of a name has been established, it should always be used in the same form throughout the catalog.

Which Name?

Occasionally an author is known by more than one name. Standard practice in libraries today is to put that name in the author heading by which the person is commonly known. Thus it should not be Carter, James Earl; Thibault, Jacques-Anatole; or Clemens, Samuel Langhorne, but Carter, Jimmy; France, Anatole; and Twain, Mark. The catalog will be easiest to use if all the works of an author are listed under the same name. Cross-references to this "official" name can be made from the author's other name or names as needed (cross-references are explained in chapter 12).

Distinguishing Between Identical Names

As catalogs grow larger it happens that different authors are encountered who have identical names. It is then necessary to add dates to names for precise identification:

    Smith, Jim, 1926-
    Smith, Jim, 1949-

Name Changes

From time to time one finds an author who has changed his or her name. There is no fixed standard procedure for handling such situations, but a good basic rule is to use the new name throughout, changing all old name headings that may be already in the catalog. A note should be added to all old cards indicating the author's current name.

Here is an author added entry:

```
658          Ike, Alice Burns.
L5           Literature of business and finance /
             Alice Burns Ike. -- Los Angeles :
             Price Publications, 1970.
             240 p.
```

Here is the entry after the name has changed:

```
658          Grigsby, Alice
L5           Literature of business and finance /
             Alice Burns Ike. -- Los Angeles :
             Price Publications, 1970.
             240 p.


             Author's current name: Alice Grigsby.
```

In some cases it will be helpful to make a see reference from
the old name to the current name. One could, of course,
leave old books under the old name and place the new books
under the current name. But the result would be a confusing
catalog.

Form of Personal Author Heading

     If an author's name consists of more than one part, such as a given name and a surname, that part of the name is typed first by which the added entry is to be filed. This is known as a question of "form of heading." Notice that in the example on page 71 Gilbert Lew's name was inverted for the heading: "Lew, Gilbert." Inversion of the name has the effect of arranging all such entries under the surnames. But notice that not all two-part names need to be inverted. The added entry for the Indian author Taverekere Srikantaiah's book would carry a heading in this form: "Taverekere, Srikantaiah." This is so because Indian names customarily give the surname first.

     Names with separately written prefixes can pose problems for the cataloger. A good basic rule is to treat all prefixes as part of the name. Thus the author heading for John van der Mitten appears as Van der Mitten, John. The heading for Beulah de los Grandes is De los Grandes, Beulah. The heading for the corporate author Los Altos City Museum is just that, Los Altos City Museum. Unfortunately, the customs vary from country to country and it is not always easy to know if the prefix should be part of the name or not; for example, should it be Bodlien, Gertrud von, or Von Bodlien, Gertrud? The cataloger may have to consult reference sources and possibly make cross references from the form of the name not used.

     Care must also be taken with double names. The American writer John Crow Ransom is entered as "Ransom, John Crow". But the British statesman David Lloyd George becomes "Lloyd George, David." Spanish names often present similar difficulties. The poet Federico Garcia Lorca, very often just referred to as "Lorca," is actually "Garcia Lorca, Federico." But Juan Nicasio Gallego is "Gallego, Juan Nicasio." In case of doubt, biographical reference sources must be consulted to establish the correct form of a name.

CORPORATE AUTHOR ENTRIES

     Some publications are issued by corporate agencies rather than by individually named people. Here is an example:

Added entry (corporate author)

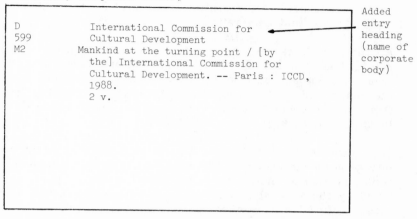

```
 D              International Commission for
 599            Cultural Development
 M2             Mankind at the turning point / [by
                the] International Commission for
                Cultural Development. -- Paris : ICCD,
                1988.
                2 v.
```

Added
entry
heading
(name of
corporate
body)

This so-called corporate author added entry is made for the
benefit of the library user who might know only the name
of the issuing agency or who wants to know which publications
of this organization are owned by the library.

Form of Corporate Author Headings

On the question of form in corporate author headings
whole volumes could be written. Suffice it to say that there
are two ways to construct a corporate name heading. One
can take the name as it is presented in the publication itself
on the title page and show it in that form in the added entry
heading. This may lead to inconsistent entries in the catalog,
however, because different publications by the same agency
may not show the agency's name in the same form every time.

A second method is to show the name of the agency in
a standardized form, regardless of how it is presented in the
publication. Such standardized corporate names often are laid
out in a hierarchical pattern. A government agency's name,
for example, usually begins with the name of the jurisdiction,
followed by the names of lesser units:

New York (City). Police Department.

or

United States. Congress. Senate. Committee on the
Judiciary. Subcommittee on Federal Charters, Holi-
days, and Celebrations.

All the lines in the last example are one agency's name. A
helpful book for determining the hierarchical relationships
among various agencies of the United States government is
the annual United States Government Manual published by the
Office of the Federal Register and sold by the Government
Printing Office, Washington, DC   20402.

Sometimes the full name of a corporate agency is divided
into so many sub-agencies that one may want to eliminate the
middle portion of the name, giving only the largest unit followed by the smallest subdivision that can stand alone without
being confused with another agency. Thus, instead of writing

North Caledonia. Dept. of Transportation. Div. of
Highways.

one may use this heading,

North Caledonia. Div. of Highways.

there being only one Division of Highways in the state of North
Caledonia. The most important principle in establishing corporate author headings is consistency. If a name is once established as, say, "New York (City). Police Department,"
then all publications emanating from that department should be
kept together under the same heading. If the principle of
consistency or "name authority" control is disregarded, the
file of police department documents will soon become widely
dispersed under such headings as "City of New York.   Police
Department," "Police Department of the City of New York,"
"New York Police," and other possible variants of the name.

Entry of publications under jurisdictions, such as North
Caledonia. Div. of Highways, is going out of fashion. Whenever a name can stand alone it should be used without the
name of the superior agency. Thus it is "Library of Congress," not "United States. Library of Congress."

In an ideal situation one would make cross-references
from all names not used to the names used. In some libraries
special card files, so-called authority files, are maintained

where a record is kept of which personal and corporate names
have been used.

Here is an example of a corporate name that would probably deserve a cross-reference. If a publication is cataloged
under the author heading

Teamsters' Union

then, under the principle of name authority, the next publication from this group should also be entered under that name.
To help people that might be looking for the full name of the
organization, a cross reference should be made:

```
            International Brotherhood of
            Teamsters, Chauffeurs, Warehouse-
            men and Helpers of America
            see
            Teamsters' Union
```

More on cross-references in chapter 12.

Corporate Author Plus Uniform Title

In some fields, such as law and political science, it often
happens that publications of a certain type must be assembled
in the catalog under the name of a jurisdiction and further
arranged by type of publication, as for example "laws" in a
legal library or a corporate library. The type of law, in such
a library, becomes a uniform title which is added to the heading as a second added entry paragraph under the name of the
jurisdiction as corporate author, in brackets. Inclusion of

uniform titles in this fashion insures that all editions of the
California agricultural code, for example, stand together in
the catalog, no matter what the actual titles of the editions
may be:

```
630          California
C2           [Agricultural Code]
A5b          Bancmester's California Codes :
             Agriculture / edited by...
```

```
630          California
C2           [Agricultural Code]
A5j          Jones' California agricultural code. --
             12th ed. -- San Jose, CA : Jones
             Publishing Co., 1980.
             290 p.
```

```
610          California
C2           [Health and Safety Code]
H3b          Bancmester's California Codes :
             Health and Safety / edited by...
```

Here is another example of corporate author plus uniform title added entries and how they keep certain types of works together in the catalog. Suppose there were three books in the library containing the constitution of the United States, entitled Our Constitution, America's Basic Law, and Understanding the Constitution. The following added entries will display the three together (location codes, physical descriptions, and notes not shown):

```
KF            United States
4525          [Constitution]
G6            America's basic law / [ed. by]
                 Joe Doe. -- New York : Glaubers,
                 1970.
```

```
KF            United States
4527          [Constitution]
L2            Our constitution / by Jane Allin. --
                 Boston : Lance Publications, 1975.
```

```
KF            United States
2528          [Constitution]
B8            Understanding the constitution /
                 [by] Enid Brock. -- Chicago :
                 Folley, 1967.
```

NO AUTHOR ADDED ENTRIES

Not all publications need author entries. Periodicals,
for example, such as Time or the New Yorker, cannot be said
to have personal authors and no author added entries are
made, regardless of how well-known the editor may be.

TITLE ADDED ENTRIES

Occasionally the title given on the title page of a publication, and therefore leading the bibliographic description,
the "natural" title, is not what library users are likely to look
for.

Whenever different editions of a work bear different
titles, it may be necessary to collect them together in the
catalog by a uniform title. Take the case of The Tragedy of
Hamlet, Prince of Denmark, by William Shakespeare. Not many
library patrons will look for this book under T for Tragedy.
Instead they will look for the shortened popular or "uniform"
title, "Hamlet." That is why an added entry for that uniform
title is made, again in the same added entry format:

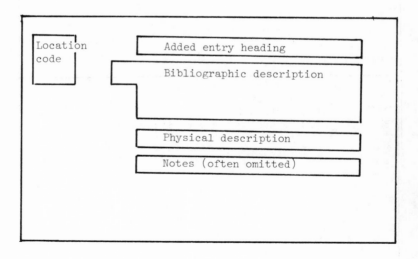

Here is the completed example:

```
822.33      [Hamlet]
H2          Tragedy of Hamlet, Prince of Denmark /
D7              by William Shakespeare ; ed. by Joe
                Doe. -- Chicago : Willaman, 1920.
                200 p.
```

By this stratagem all editions of the play are listed together in the catalog:

```
PR
2807        Hamlet and Julius Caesar : two
X7              Shakespearean tragedies for the
                modern reader... 1980.
```

```
PR          [Hamlet]
2807        Tragedy of Hamlet, Prince of Denmark /
Y6              by William Shakespeare ; ed. by...
                1970.
```

```
PR
2807        Hamlet / William Shakespeare. --
Z5              London : Agee, 1958.
```

Or take these two entries:

842 S2 H7e	[Huis clos] No exit / Jean-paul Sartre ; tr. by Joe Doe. -- New York : Crofts, 1980.

842 S2 H7	Huis clos / Jean-Paul Sartre. -- Paris : Proche, 1970.

The uniform title keeps these two versions of the play together.

Here is another example, a book entitled The Holy Bible.
Few people would look for it in the catalog under H for Holy;
instead, they will look for the uniform title "Bible." An
example of an appropriate entry follows.

220 H7	[Bible] Holy Bible containing the old and new testaments / edited by James Dorn. -- Philadelphia : Grosch, 1940. 500 p.

With the uniform title the cataloger brings together all the
versions of the Bible that the library may own, regardless of
whether the books are entitled Holy Bible, New English Bible,
Modern Bible, or whatever.

Uniform titles are not phenomena that occur in the real
world of books.   Uniform titles are not found on the title pages
of books.   They are made up by librarians on the basis of
presumed reader needs and certain conventions.   There are
few generally binding principles.   Catalogers make these decisions from case to case, supported by precedent as found in
previous cataloging, reference books, bibliographies, rule
books, and other libraries' catalogs.   As in all other phases
of cataloging, consistency is of the essence in the establish-
ment of uniform titles.   The cataloger who decides to enter one
of Shakespeare's plays under the uniform title should be consistent and do it for all of Shakespeare's plays whose natural
titles begin with non-significant words.   If Tragedy of Hamlet
becomes [Hamlet], then First Part of King Henry the Fourth
might become [Henry IV, Part I] and Comedy of Much Ado
about Nothing could turn into [Much Ado about Nothing],
and so on.   Notice, though, that a title such as Comedy of
Errors requires no uniform title added entry.   This natural
title cannot be improved by arbitrary shortening.   Likewise,
if a book containing the play Hamlet has the natural title
Hamlet, it does not also need the uniform title [Hamlet].
Notice also the convention to enclose all uniform titles in
brackets.   This indicates that the information was not found in
the publication but supplied by the cataloger.   And notice,
finally, that a uniform title supplements the natural title.   It
does not take its place, no matter how unlikely it may be that
readers will look for the natural title.

Keyword Title Entries

Some natural titles begin with nondistinctive words,
such as "Introduction to..." or "Dictionary of...," that are
often not exactly remembered by library users.   Keywords
that appear further inside the title, however, are more easily
remembered.   This is why it is sometimes a good idea to make
added entries for keyword titles.   Here is an example:

```
001.6        String BASIC
I6           Introduction to string BASIC / by
             Hazel Grant. -- New York : Grau,
             1976.
```

TRACINGS

All added entries must be traced on the main entry.
Author tracings are by convention numbered in Roman numerals. Thus, the tracing for the added entry shown on page 71
might read:

I. Lew, Gilbert.

The tracing for the corporate author added entry shown on
page 77 might read:

I. International Commission for Cultural Development.

Here is the tracing for the topmost heading shown on page
80:

I. California. (Agricultural Code).

The reason for tracings is this: once an added entry is made
and filed away, it passes out of the cataloger's consciousness
unless a careful record is maintained. And since it is highly
undesirable to have unknown and uncontrolled entries in the
catalog, a complete record of all added entries is kept on each
main entry. By means of this record the cataloger can trace
all added entries, whence the name "tracings" for this bit
of housekeeping information kept on the main entry.

If the last copy of a book is removed from the library by loss or weeding, the main entry must be removed from the catalog, of course. The tracings at the foot of the main entry remind the cataloger also to pull all added entries out of the catalog, or to "pull the tracings," as the jargon goes. If this step is forgotten, blind references remain in the catalog, cards for which there are no books.

Each tracing, by the way, specifies exactly the information that has been given in the added entry heading.

Complete and reliable records must be kept for title added entries, too. For each title added entry that is made a suitable tracing is added at the foot of the main entry. Title tracings follow author tracings. They are numbered in Roman numerals with the word "Title:" added. Here are two main entries complete with tracings:

```
220
H7          Holy Bible containing the old and new
               testaments / edited by James Dorn. --
               Philadelphia : Grosch, 1940.
               500 p.




I. Dorn, James, ed.  II. Title: [Bible]
```

```
001.6
I6          Introduction to string BASIC / by
               Hazel Grant. -- New York : Grau,
               1976.




1. BASIC (COMPUTER PROGRAM LANGUAGE)  I. Grant,
Hazel.  II. Title: String BASIC.
```

Chapter 9

CATEGORICAL ADDED ENTRIES _____

Author and title added entries serve those library users who are looking for a publication of which they know the author or the title.

Many library users, however, take a different approach. They will be looking for any suitable publication on a certain subject or of a certain kind. They do not know the names of authors or the titles of any particular publications. They look for publications that fall into certain categories. A different kind of added entry is provided for such readers, the categorical added entry. There are three kinds of categorical added entries: subject added entries, genre added entries, and format added entries. By tradition, all three kinds are often referred to as "subject" headings, even those that do not designate subjects. I prefer the inclusive term "categorical added entry."

Categorical added entries are made in the same format as author and title added entries.

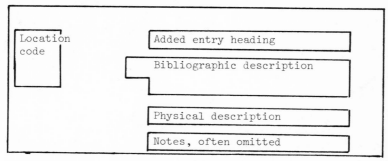

SUBJECT ADDED ENTRIES

Most categorical entries are made for the subject of books. All books (and of course also all other media) that have to do with, say, organic chemistry can be described by an added entry that carries a suitable subject heading, such as

CHEMISTRY, ORGANIC

in the added entry heading.

Here is an example of a subject added entry record:

Added entry (subject)

```
615.3      CHEMISTRY, ORGANIC ◄───────────────────
C7         Chemistry of organic medical products /
           by Glenn L. Jenkins [and] Walter
           Herting. -- 3rd ed. -- New York :
           Culver, 1975.
           499 p.
```

Added entry heading (subject heading)

By convention, subject headings are typed in all upper case letters.

Here is another example, a book entitled Barrow, Pyramid, and Tomb, by Leslie V. Grinsell. It deals with tombs. An added entry is made under the subject heading TOMBS. For readers who are looking for a slightly different aspect of the subject, another added entry can be made for the same book under the subject heading FUNERAL RITES AND CEREMONIES.

Subject terminology used in headings must be controlled to remain useful. It will not do to simply invent subject headings on the spot. There are too many words in the English language to guarantee any semblance of consistency and uniformity in an uncontrolled subject heading vocabulary.

The same cataloger working on the book by Grinsell, for
example, could on another day have assigned the heading
GRAVES. To a similar book the heading CRYPTS might be
given. A prospective reader interested in burial practices
would never find all the relevant books unless he or she
could think of all similar headings. To prevent scattering of
related materials under different terms many libraries control
their subject heading vocabulary by using a published general
schedule such as the Sears List of Subject Headings or the
Library of Congress Subject Headings. Many specialized lists
are available also, such as Medical Subject Headings, published
by the National Library of Medicine, the Thesaurus of Engineering
and Scientific Terms, published by the Engineers Joint Council,
the INSPEC Thesaurus, published by the British Institution of
Electrical Engineers, and many others.

Here is a sample entry copied from the Sears List of
Subject Headings:

> Tombs 726
>   See also Brasses; Catacombs;
>   Cemeteries; Epitaphs; Mounds
>   and Mound builders
>   x Burial; Graves; Mausoleums;
>   Rock tombs; Sepulchers;
>   Vaults (Sepulchral)
>   xx Archeology; Architecture;
>   Cemeteries; Monuments; Shrines

This entry tells the cataloger that Tombs is an approved
subject heading. The number 726 is the suggested Dewey
Decimal Classification section for tombs. The see also paragraph suggests to the cataloger that the five headings listed,
Brasses, Catacombs, Cemeteries, Epitaphs, and Mounds and
Mound builders, might be considered instead of Tombs, for
the book in hand.

The see also, x, and xx paragraphs in the Sears List
example have to do with cross-references, references from certain headings to other headings in the catalog. Cross references will be discussed in chapter 12.

Occasionally, printed subject heading lists contain scope
notes to help the cataloger choose the proper heading. Here
is an example, also from the Sears List:

Maps 912
Use for general materials about maps and their history.
Materials on the methods of map making and the
mapping of areas are entered under Map drawing.
Collections of maps of several countries are entered
under Atlases.

Here is an entry copied from the INSPEC Thesaurus:

Internal combustion engines
NT two cycle engines
BT engines
RT ignition
starting

The abbreviations stand for narrower term (NT), broader term
(BT), and related term (RT). The idea is to help the cataloger select the best fitting subject heading for the book in
hand. Thesauri also sometimes add scope notes. This example
is from INSPEC Thesaurus:

mechanical variables control
this heading is restricted to those variables which
are not covered by other specific headings. See
also, for example, force control; thickness control;
velocity control; vibration control.

The Sears List heading shown above is a single-word
heading. But because of the fine nuances of meaning in the
English language, many subjects must be expressed in several
words. Here are some examples: GLASS FIBERS, FORCE AND
ENERGY, FORGERY OF WORKS OF ART, GRANTS-IN-AID,
BLACKS IN LITERATURE AND ART.

Single-word and multi-word headings can be in the
singular (FOOTBALL, GLASS FIBER) or, often with different
meaning, in the plural (TOMBS, GLASS FIBERS).

By convention, some multi-word headings are given in
direct order (MUNICIPAL FINANCE, AMERICAN LITERATURE),
others are inverted (FINANCE, PERSONAL, OR ART, AMERI-
CAN). Some multi-word headings are given as phrases (ART
INDUSTRIES AND TRADE), others consist of a heading with
a subdivision (ART--GALLERIES AND MUSEUMS). Such in-
consistencies occur in many lists of subject headings. They

must be dealt with as they occur.   They cannot be "learned"
since there is no logic behind them.

When using lists of subject descriptors such as the
Thesaurus of Engineering and Scientific Terms already mentioned above, the cataloger finds that many terms in such lists
are single concept terms.   Consider a book that explains how
to fly a helicopter.   In the Sears List of Subject Headings
a conveniently precoordinated heading will be found that ex-
presses the subject of the book in one term: HELICOPTERS--
PILOTING.   In the Thesaurus of Engineering and Scientific
Terms, however, there is no such heading.   The cataloger
will probably do best by assigning two separate terms, HELI-
COPTERS and PILOT TRAINING.   One card, then, will be
filed under H, the other under P.   The person looking for
material on flying helicopters can look under HELICOPTERS
and scan all the titles listed there for books that deal with
piloting, or else look under PILOT TRAINING and see if any
books specifically devoted to helicopters are listed.   If tracings
are maintained on all entries, the catalog user can simplify
the search by scanning all tracings for the companion term.
Here is the picture of a card that would lead to a relevant
book in this fictitious search:

```
629            HELICOPTERS
F5             Flying the HFG-200 helicopter :
               a manual for student pilots /
               by George Doe. -- New York :
               Grey, 1988.
               399 p.




1. HELICOPTERS.   2. PILOT TRAINING.   I. Doe,
George.
```

Even with the help of published lists, however, the assignment of subject headings to publications is very difficult
work.   In one large American library the fifth edition of a
book entitled Abnormal Psychology and Modern Life, for ex-

ample, was given the subject heading PSYCHIATRY. But the sixth edition of the same book cannot be found under that heading. It was entered under PSYCHOLOGY, PATHOLOGICAL. This shows how difficult it is to be consistent, even for highly skilled and experienced librarians.

Not all publications have a subject. Beethoven's Pastoral Symphony recorded in a publication called RCA Victor LM 2114, for example, is neither about pastors nor about symphonies. It is not about music, either. It is not about anything; it simply is music. Such a publication needs no subject heading.

Also, not all subjects are topics. A book about the painter Henri Matisse, for example, is not about something but about someone. It needs a subject heading like this:

MATISSE, HENRI

Since it is hard to predict about whom books will be written, there is, of course, no published master list of name subject headings. The cataloger makes them up on the spot, taking care to be consistent in form and spelling. Thus, if a book about Igor Chernov gets the subject heading CHERNOV, IGOR, then a second book about the same person should have the same heading, not some variant such as TCHERNOV or CHERNOW.

Some books are about other books. Typically, the subject heading for such an item consists of the name of the author plus the title of the book that is the subject. A book discussing Darwin's Origin of Species gets this subject heading:

DARWIN, CHARLES ROBERT, 1809-1882. ON THE ORIGIN OF SPECIES BY MEANS OF NATURAL SELECTION.

Such author/title subject headings, too, will not be found in any list. They must be made up as needed and this should be done in a consistent fashion. The same goes for uniform title subject headings. A book about the Bible, for example, gets the subject heading BIBLE. Note well that a book entitled The New American Bible, containing the text of the Bible, gets a title added entry under the heading "Bible." It does not get a subject added entry under BIBLE because it is the Bible, and is not about the Bible!

Like classification, subject heading work requires a thorough understanding of the field of knowledge represented by the library's collection. There is no shortcut possible because the task requires two fundamental steps that cannot be simplified: first, an examination of the publication in hand to determine what it is about (which takes knowledge and experience), and second, the selection of suitable terms to express the subject content in such a way that all publications dealing in a similar way with the same topics will always carry the same subject headings and that the headings chosen are the best ones for the library's clientele (which takes more knowledge, experience, and a thorough familiarity with the schedule of headings used, with the library's holdings, and with the needs of the library's users).

If the cataloger lacks the subject knowledge or necessary experience and cannot enlist the help of an expert, it is far better to defer the making of subject added entries, or even to abandon the project altogether, than to waste time and energy on the childish exercise of listing, in a medical library, a book entitled Introduction to the Medical Profession under the subject heading MEDICINE, or in a church library, a book on St. Paul under RELIGION. Far better not to have a subject catalog than a poorly done subject catalog that lists books under topics and aspects of topics that they don't really deal with, or fails to list important publications under the key subjects that they do deal with.

However, the person appointed to operate a small library often has no power in such decisions. Administrators, having little expertise as far as library work is concerned, cannot be relied upon to appreciate the complexities of subject cataloging. To them it seems a simple task that has to be done. A compromise solution must therefore be found. Here are a few pointers, then, on how to go about assigning subject headings to books and other publications.

First, adopt a published master list of subject headings. Get help and advice from the American Library Association, the Special Library Association, the Medical Library Association, or any other suitable professional organization in the field (refer also to the remarks on page 21).

Second, take the publication to be cataloged and study the table of contents (if it is a book), the label (if it is a

phonograph record, cassette, or similar medium), the preface,
introduction, blurb, or whatever summary information about
the publication is available. Determine if the publication can
be said to be "about" anything.

Third, if a publication can be said to have a subject,
determine if the whole publication is about one well-defined
subject, or about several separate subjects, or about several
sub-topics of one general subject. If the publication contains
several distinct works, determine if they all deal with the
same subject or with several separate subjects.

Fourth, if the publication deals with one subject assign
to it from the master list the narrowest term that character-
izes the subject. Thus, a book devoted entirely to the be-
havior of sheep is given the narrow subject heading

   SHEEP--BEHAVIOR

not the broad heading SHEEP.

The cataloger must avoid assigning general subject
headings in addition to specific ones. A book dealing with
the history of twentieth-century sculpture carries one specific
heading

   SCULPTURE--HISTORY--20TH CENTURY

It should not also be listed under SCULPTURE--HISTORY and
under SCULPTURE. The entries would file close to each other,
leading to unnecessary redundancy.

Fifth, if the publication or the works contained in it
deal with a small number of separate subjects for which no
comprehensive term exists, assign the narrowest possible
term for each of the components of the topic. Thus for a
book about sheep and swine assign two headings, SHEEP and
SWINE, since there is no collective name for these two kinds
of animals.

Sixth, a book dealing with many sub-topics of a general
topic poses a problem. Consider a book dealing with bricks,
cement, concrete, stone, structural steel, wallboard, and
wood, in so many chapters. A subject entry could be made
under the heading BRICKS. But this would be misleading

since the book does not deal with one sole subject, bricks.
Only one chapter is about bricks. A better, more logical
strategy is to enter this book under a summary term that
comprises bricks, cement, concrete, etc. One term that
covers all these materials would be

BUILDING MATERIALS

Of course, this broad summary heading does not help the
person with a special interest in bricks. For that reader a
so-called subject analytic added entry would be fine, under
the heading

BRICKS, chapter 1 of

The analytic tells the reader exactly what to expect: only
one chapter in the book is on bricks. Needless to say, such
analytics are costly in time taken for design, production, and
filing. They are therefore seldom made. But more on analytics in chapter 10.

Often so much material accumulates under a heading that
it must be subdivided to provide a finer breakdown of the
topic. Subject headings are often subdivided by other subjects (PHILOSOPHY--HISTORY). They can also be subdivided
by region (ART--ITALY), by genre (ITALY--FICTION), or
by format (LINGUISTICS--ATLASES).

History headings are often more complex. History books
are first divided into countries or regions, subdivided by the
word "History":

EUROPE--HISTORY

UNITED STATES--HISTORY

For finer distinctions, history is then divided into time periods
by means of so-called chronological subdivisions. Chronological
subdivisions, published as all other subdivisions in the Sears
List and in similar aids, are tailored to the country under discussion. The years 1492 and 1648, for example, are important
landmarks in the history of Europe. Books dealing with historical aspects of the Renaissance and the Reformation, therefore, may be assigned a three-part subject heading, like:

EUROPE--HISTORY--1492-1648

That same time period is not meaningful in the context of the history of the United States. Here, books might deal with the Revolution:

UNITED STATES--HISTORY--REVOLUTION, 1775-1783

Revolutions, of course, have happened elsewhere, but at different times. Thus the catalog may have other headings that follow the same pattern:

FRANCE--HISTORY--REVOLUTION, 1791-1797

ITALY--HISTORY--REVOLUTION OF 1848

Occasionally, still further refinements are needed, such as:

ITALY--HISTORY--REVOLUTION OF 1848--FICTION

But small libraries ought to keep headings as simple as possible. Often the only reason for subdivisions is to divide large blocks of like headings into meaningful groups. If the library has only a few things on a topic, two- and three-part headings are a nuisance to the catalog user, not a help.

To sum up: a subject heading answers the question, Is this a publication or work about something or someone?

GENRE ADDED ENTRIES

Some books are looked for because they contain literature of a certain genre. Here is a genre added entry for a collection of stories:

```
808.83     SHORT STORIES
W7         World treasury of short fiction /
             ed. by Joe Doe. -- Boston :
             Gremlin, 1921.
             480 p.
```

Since the heading here designates the genre of literature contained in the book cataloged, not the subject of the book,
this type of heading cannot rightly be called a subject heading.
It would best be called a genre heading.

Genre added entries are easier to make than subject
added entries because the available choice of terms is much
smaller. There is only a very limited number of genres to be
considered. But genre headings, too, must be controlled to
prevent inconsistency. Published lists of subject headings
can be used for guidance. They usually contain many genre
headings. This fact is not well advertised, although the distinction between subject and genre is often made. The 12th
edition of the Sears List of Subject Headings, for example,
has this entry under SHORT STORY:

> SHORT STORY 808.3
> Use for materials on the technique of short story
> writing. Collections of short stories are entered
> under SHORT STORIES

Clearly, this note implies a difference between subject and
genre heading, even if the nature of the difference is not
spelled out. Unfortunately, the distinction is not carried
through consistently. Thus there are no term pairs like
poetry/poems or drama/plays in the Sears List. For uniformity and clarity it is recommended that, in literature, plain
headings be interpreted as genre headings. Let SHORT
STORIES be assigned to a publication that contains short
stories. Let AMERICAN POETRY be assigned to an anthology
of American poetry. Let DRAMA be assigned to a book that
contains plays.

Should a book, however, contain essays about the
drama or about individual plays, use the heading with a suitable subdivision:

DRAMA--HISTORY AND CRITICISM

Likewise, the heading GERMAN POETRY stands for a book
that contains poems. The heading GERMAN POETRY--HISTORY
AND CRITICISM is for a book that contains essays about German poetry.

Genre headings such as SHORT STORIES or DRAMA are

usually assigned only to items that contain many works of that genre. If a book contains just one story, and there are such books, it is not customary to make a genre added entry, although that would be a logical thing to do if one were interested in the retrieval of works of that genre. In the age of the card catalog it simply was not feasible. This improvement can be achieved more readily by the use of a computer, where available.

Since the number of genre headings is small as compared to the vast body of subject headings, it is feasible to make up one's own system. Terms used should be recorded in a list. Similar terms not used should be tied into this list with cross-references, as in the following example:

DRAMA

ESSAYS

PLAYS see DRAMA

SHORT STORIES

In many libraries literature headings must be subdivided by nationality. Most published lists confuse the concepts of nationality and language. AMERICAN DRAMA, for example, usually means plays written by Americans. But SPANISH DRAMA can mean plays written by Spaniards, by South Americans, or even plays written in or translated into Spanish. If possible, be consistent. Let American, English, Spanish, Mexican, etc. be ethnic adjectives when they modify genres. Use parenthetical qualifiers to indicate language, but only if necessary:

SWISS DRAMA (FRENCH)

but

MEXICAN DRAMA

Catalogers making their own list of genre headings should also be consistent in respect to format. Let it be either

AMERICAN POETRY
AMERICAN ESSAYS
AMERICAN SHORT STORIES

or inverted

> POETRY, AMERICAN
> ESSAYS, AMERICAN
> SHORT STORIES, AMERICAN

Of course, when a published list is used consistency may be
unattainable. The prestigious Library of Congress Subject
Headings, for example, mixes straight and inverted forms,
giving AMERICAN POETRY, but SHORT STORIES, AMERICAN.

Ambiguity

To avoid ambiguity one must see to it that each categorical heading serves only one function. As we have noted,
in the Sears List of Subject Headings the term SHORT STORY
(singular) stands for the topic, while SHORT STORIES (plural) stands for the genre, for collections of short stories.
Ideally, no one term should be made to serve both purposes.

If a published list furnishes an ambiguous term, such
as (from the Sears List of Subject Headings)

> PIANO MUSIC

which could be a subject (a book about piano music) or a
genre (an actual piece of music written for the piano), it
will be best to qualify the headings. A cumbersome but effective method would be to mark true subject headings with
a parenthetical qualifier, such as

> PIANO MUSIC (TOPIC)

and genre headings

> PIANO MUSIC (GENRE)

Alternately, one could make it a rule to qualify only subjects
and assume that unqualified headings are genre headings.
Thus the heading PIANO MUSIC would say "this is piano
music," while the book about piano music carries the heading
PIANO MUSIC (TOPIC).

In one large computer-based bibliographic network of

research libraries, this problem has been solved by establishing different files. When split into separate files, a book
about piano music will be listed in the file BOOKS; a book
that contains pieces of piano music transcribed in musical notation will be in the file SCORES. By searching the file
SCORES and the categorical heading PIANO MUSIC, one will
then retrieve, by definition, only works of the genre piano
music. Looking for PIANO MUSIC in the file BOOKS, on the
other hand, will retrieve only writings about piano music.

To sum up: a genre heading answers the question,
Does this publication <u>contain</u> works of a certain kind?

FORMAT ADDED ENTRIES

Format added entries are for books that can be said
to be of a certain format. They differ from genre added entries as well as from subject added entries. Here is an example:

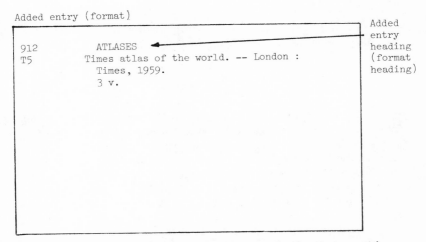

Added entry (format)

```
912        ATLASES  ◄───────────
T5         Times atlas of the world. -- London :
           Times, 1959.
           3 v.
```

Added
entry
heading
(format
heading)

Since the book cataloged is not a book about atlases, this
added entry cannot be called a subject added entry. Since
the book does not contain any atlases, it cannot be called a
genre added entry, either. Instead, the book <u>is</u> an atlas.
It is a member of the category "collections of maps," and has
the format of an atlas. This added entry, therefore, would
best be called a format added entry.

Just as subject and genre headings must be controlled,
format headings also must be taken from a published or homemade list that refers the user from terms not used to those
that are used. Here is an example from a homemade list of
format headings:

DICTIONARIES--FOREIGN LANGUAGE

LABORATORY MANUALS

UNABRIDGED DICTIONARIES see DICTIONARIES--
ENGLISH LANGUAGE

The cross-reference UNABRIDGED DICTIONARIES see
DICTIONARIES--ENGLISH LANGUAGE reminds the cataloger
that no heading exists in the system for unabridged dictionaries.

Published lists of subject headings, of course, contain
many format headings. However, they are never marked as
such and are intermingled with true subject headings. One
has to be very watchful.

To sum up: a format heading answers the question,
Is this publication of a certain format?

TRACINGS

As in the case of author and title added entries, tracings
for categorical headings must be maintained at the foot of the
corresponding main entries. Categorical tracings are traditionally numbered with Arabic numerals and precede all other
tracings. Categorical tracings repeat the information contained
in the heading and are typed in all capitals. Here is the
tracing for the heading shown on page 89.

1. CHEMISTRY, ORGANIC

Here is the tracing for the genre heading on page 97.

1. SHORT STORIES

Unless the function of the categorical heading is indicated by
parenthetical qualifiers, as in PIANO MUSIC (TOPIC), the
distinction between subject, genre, and format is not indicated
in the tracings.

   Here is a main entry for an atlas, complete with format tracing:

Main entry

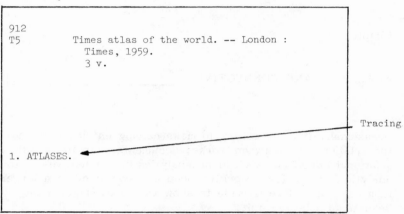

912
T5   Times atlas of the world. -- London :
     Times, 1959.
     3 v.

                           Tracing

1. ATLASES.

Chapter 10

ANALYTICS AND CONNECTIVES _____

Occasionally it is necessary to make catalog entries that show
the relationships between works, documents, and items. Such
relational added entries can be analytics or connectives. An
analytic is made for a work or document contained in a larger
item. A connective is made to show that a cataloged item
belongs to a larger unit.

WORK ANALYTICS

Many items contain more than one work. A phonograph
record may contain several works of music. Work analytics,
often just called analytics, can be made for them. Here is
an example:

Analytic added entry

```
Phono        Holberg Suite, in ◄──────────────────   Added
388          Peer Gynt suite, No. 1 [and other         entry
             music] / by Grieg. -- New                 heading
             York : Vance, 1965.
             Sound disc : 33 1/3 rpm.

             Vance V-661
```

Here is an analytic for a work contained in a multi-volume set of books:

Analytic added entry

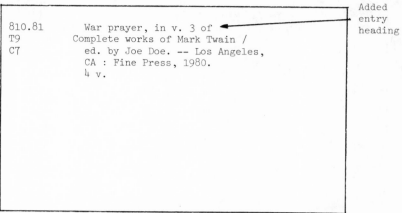

Added
entry
heading

```
810.81        War prayer, in v. 3 of
T9            Complete works of Mark Twain /
C7                ed. by Joe Doe. -- Los Angeles,
              CA : Fine Press, 1980.
              4 v.
```

The two analytics shown above are work title analytics. Sometimes it is desirable to show an analyzed work under the author's name. This requires an author/title analytic. Here is an example:

Analytic added entry (author/title)

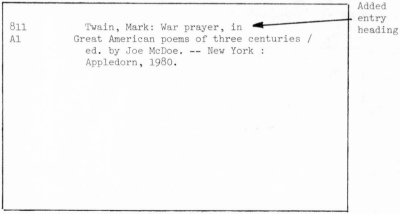

Added
entry
heading

```
811           Twain, Mark: War prayer, in
A1            Great American poems of three centuries /
                  ed. by Joe McDoe. -- New York :
              Appledorn, 1980.
```

Title/author analytics are also possible, as shown in the example on the next page.

Analytic added entry (title/author)

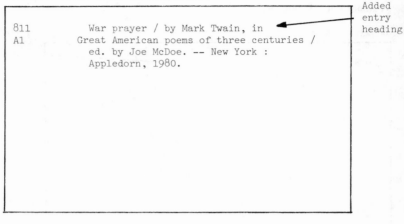

Added
entry
heading

```
811            War prayer / by Mark Twain, in
A1             Great American poems of three centuries /
               ed. by Joe McDoe. -- New York :
               Appledorn, 1980.
```

Tracings for Work Analytics

Like all other added entries, analytics must be traced
at the foot of the main entry. Tracings for author and title
analytics are numbered in Roman numerals. Here are the
tracings on the Peer Gynt main entry. The abbreviation
TANAL stands for title analytic:

Main entry

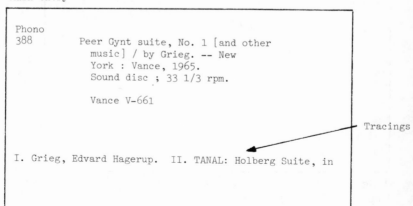

Tracings

```
Phono
388            Peer Gynt suite, No. 1 [and other
               music] / by Grieg. -- New
               York : Vance, 1965.
               Sound disc ; 33 1/3 rpm.

               Vance V-661



I. Grieg, Edvard Hagerup.  II. TANAL: Holberg Suite, in
```

The tracings, it should be noted, repeat the information that
is given in the heading, including the word "in."

DOCUMENT ANALYTICS

If a multi-volume set is cataloged as a unit (i.e., under
the set description principle), analytics may be needed to
direct readers to the individual documents. Here is an example:

Main entry

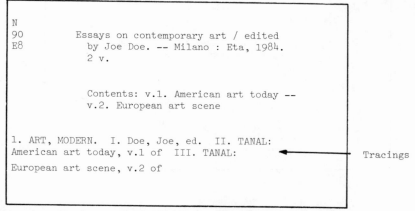

Tracings

Tracing II, for example, leads to the following analytic:

Analytic added entry

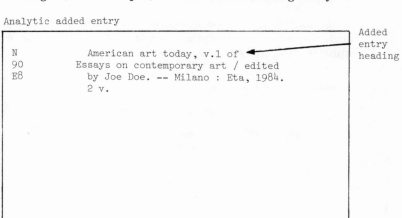

Added
entry
heading

Since this kind of added entry analyzes a set in terms of its component documents, I call it a document analytic. Notice that users will now find this book under either title, "Essays on..." or "American art..."

If a multi-volume set main entry lists the contents, as in this example, some librarians will simplify their tracings as shown below:

Main entry

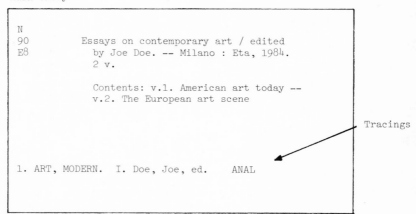

```
N
90          Essays on contemporary art / edited
E8             by Joe Doe. -- Milano : Eta, 1984.
               2 v.

               Contents: v.1. American art today --
               v.2. The European art scene
                                                              Tracings

   1. ART, MODERN.  I. Doe, Joe, ed.    ANAL
```

SUBJECT ANALYTICS

Occasionally it may be necessary to indicate the subject of a work for which an analytic is made. This can be done by a subject/title analytic. Here is an example:

Analytic added entry

```
                                                              Added
                                                              entry
523          WHITE DWARFS.  Stars, v.3 of                     heading
M7             Modern astronomy in a new key /
               edited by James Doeman. -- New
               York : Cooms, 1981.
               10 v.
```

This analytic tells the reader that important material on White
Dwarfs is found in volume 3 of this ten-volume set. To show
the tracings, here is the corresponding main entry record.
The abbreviation SANAL stands for subject analytic:

Main entry

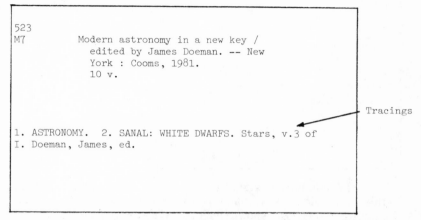

Occasionally a work contains noteworthy chapters that
need to be brought to readers' attention. A book on astron-
omy, for example, may have a chapter on Red Giants. A
chapter analytic might be helpful:

Analytic added entry

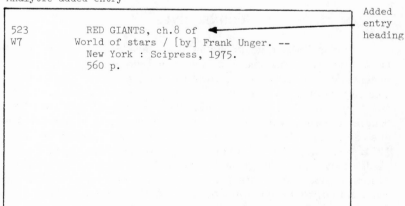

Here is the corresponding main entry, showing the tracings:

Main entry

```
523
W7        World of stars / [by] Frank Unger. --
          New York : Scipress, 1975.
          560 p.




1. STARS.  2. SANAL: RED GIANTS, ch.8 of  ←————————        Tracings
I. Unger, Frank.
```

        The labor of designing, typing, tracing, and filing ana-
lytics is considerable. That is why they are not often made.
In addition to those shown here, other methods of making
analytics exist. Whatever style a library adopts for its analytics, the cataloger must see to it that some sort of tracing
is made on the main entry so that no "blind" entries are left
in the catalog should the item ever be withdrawn.

CONNECTIVES

        If the individual books in a set are cataloged separately
(i.e. under the document description principle) it may be
necessary to connect them with the title of their parent set.
The importance of connectives is still poorly understood. In
one large American library that uses a state-of-the-art GEAC
8000 electronic online catalog, the following set stands on the
shelf: Drugs, by Richard H. Blum, 2 vols., Jossey-Bass,
1974. But in spite of several hundred thousand megabytes
of direct access storage and a powerful computer, this set
cannot be located by its title. The two component volumes
were cataloged under the document description principle as
Society and Drugs and Students and Drugs, respectively.
No connectives were made. In a small library this is easy to
fix by two simple connectives:

Analytics and Connectives

Connective added entry

```
362.2        Drugs, v.1  ◄───────────────────      Added
S7           Society and drugs / Richard H.        entry
             Blum. -- San Francisco : Jossey-      heading
             Bass, 1974.
             376 p.

             (Drugs, v.1)
```

and

Connective added entry

```
362.2        Drugs, v.2  ◄───────────────────      Added
S8           Students and drugs / Richard H.       entry
             Blum. -- San Francisco : Jossey-      heading
             Bass, 1974.
             380 p.

             (Drugs, v.2)
```

Now users will find these books either under the set title or under the individual document titles.

Tracings for Connectives

Connectives such as those shown are title added entries. They are traced as follows (the abbreviation TCON stands for title connective):

Main entry

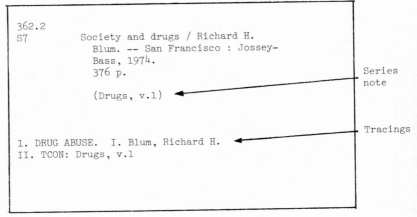

362.2
S7   Society and drugs / Richard H.
               Blum. -- San Francisco : Jossey-
               Bass, 1974.
               376 p.

               (Drugs, v.1)   Series
                                                                     note

1. DRUG ABUSE. I. Blum, Richard H.   Tracings
II. TCON: Drugs, v.1

and

Main entry

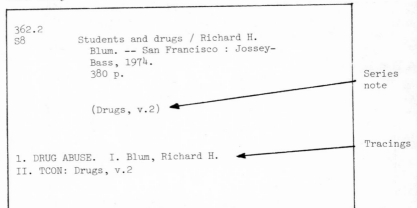

362.2
S8   Students and drugs / Richard H.
               Blum. -- San Francisco : Jossey-
               Bass, 1974.
               380 p.

                                                                     Series
                                                                     note
               (Drugs, v.2)

                                                                     Tracings
1. DRUG ABUSE. I. Blum, Richard H.
II. TCON: Drugs, v.2

Chapter 11

SHELF LIST _____

Most added entries are made for the public. They can be
called public added entries and are filed in the public catalog.
But some added entries serve the housekeeping purposes of
the library. They are kept in the librarian's work room where
they are filed by location code in the same order as the books
on the shelf, whence the name "shelf list" for this part of
the catalog.

    While public added entries are made selectively as needed
(or not at all if thought unnecessary), a shelf list entry is
made for every main entry record in the catalog, without exception. The shelf list, therefore, is the librarian's complete
record not only of what is on the shelf but of all that belongs
there.

    The shelf list is divided into as many sections as there
are different files in the library. A library that has materials
in the following three files

        Book stacks
        Reference books
        Indexes

will have a shelf list in three sections: stack shelf list,
reference shelf list, and indexes shelf list. Within each section the cards are arranged by location codes, by accession
number, by title, or however else the materials are arranged
on the shelf.

TYPOGRAPHY

The shelf list card looks very much like the main entry.
It contains the same location code, bibliographic description,
and physical description as the main entry. Notes and tracings
are omitted to gain space for housekeeping information such
as a record of copies in the collection, losses, replacements,
whether gift or purchase, date of acquisition, etc. Here is
an example of a shelf list card:

```
E
184        Chinatown, U. S. A. / by Calvin
C5            Lee. -- Garden Grove, NH :
              Doubleton, 1965.
              154 p.



gift of Dr. Marcia Blain
lost Dec 75
c.2 Mar 76
```

The housekeeping information recorded on this shelf list card
reveals that the first copy was lost and later replaced. The
library now owns one copy of this book, copy 2. If in April
1987 another copy of the same book is acquired, it receives
the same location code to which will be added the copy designation "c.3" since it is the third copy the library has owned.
On the shelf list card this information is recorded: c.3 Apr.
87. Notice that copy numbers are used only once. If copy
1 is lost or discarded, no other copy of that book will ever be
called c.1 again.

PERIODICALS RECORDS

For the holdings of periodicals and other subscriptions,
a different kind of housekeeping system is often used. Periodicals are usually weeklies or monthlies. As each issue is
received by the library the date of receipt is entered onto a

periodical record card. This is more efficient than constant
removal and handling of the shelf list card. Here is a typical
periodical record card:

Year	Vol.	J	F	M	A	M	J	J	A	S	O	N	D
1982	8 /bd	1/12	2/10	3/12	4/11	5/9	6/10	7/15	8/11	9/8	10/10	11/12	12/11
1983	9	1/11	2/12	3/10	4/13	5/11	6/8	7/10	8/14	9/11	10/12	11/15	12/7
1984	10	1/12	2/10		4/11								
North West Magazine											12/yr		

Such cards in many designs are available from library supply
houses. Many are constructed so that they can be filed flat
in shingled trays in so-called visible file or indexing cabinets.
This simplifies consultation of the list because all one has to
do is to flip up the next card to gain access to the desired
one. No removal and replacement of cards is necessary.

The example above shows that the issue for March 1984
failed to arrive and must be claimed. It also shows that the
issue for February of 1983 was lost and that vol. 8 was
bound.

FILE SPLITTERS

Occasionally, a library owns two or more copies of a
book. When one of these copies resides in one file (say, the
reference shelves) and the others elsewhere (say, the regular
stacks) a problem arises at the shelf list. For in the public
catalog all copies are represented by one main entry, and
consequently only one shelf list card is made. Yet one cannot
file one card in two places in the shelf list! The dilemma is
solved by splitting the shelf list record. One of the files is
designated as the home file (say, the reference shelves).
The shelf list card is filed in the reference shelf list. The
other file is called the alternate file. A dummy shelf list card

is made for the stack shelf list. Here is an example. First
the main entry record:

Main entry

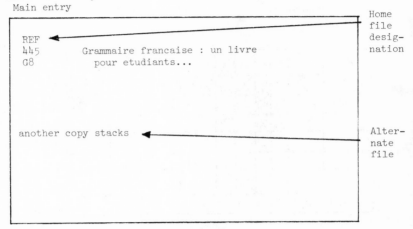

In the reference shelf list (the home file shelf list) the following shelf list card is placed:

Shelf list entry

```
REF
445          Grammaire francaise : un livre
G8               pour etudiants...




c.1
c.2 stacks



```

In the stack shelf list, the alternate file shelf list, a dummy is
placed, shown on page 117.

Second shelf list entry

```
┌─────────────────────────────────────────────────────────┐
│  445                                       dummy SL       │
│  G8          Grammaire francaise : un livre              │
│                 pour etudiants...                         │
│                                                           │
│                                                           │
│                                  for full info            │
│                                  see REF                  │
│                                      445                  │
│                                      G8                   │
│  c.2                                                      │
│                                                           │
│                                                           │
│                                                           │
│                                                           │
└─────────────────────────────────────────────────────────┘
```

Now the housekeeping records are complete and clear. While
the title was cataloged only once, every copy of the book is
represented by its shelf list card.

FILE STRADDLERS

When the parts of a series straddle two or more files,
a similar procedure will keep the shelf list records organized.
Here is the main entry for such a set:

Main entry   Home
                                                          file
                                                          desig-
                                                          nation

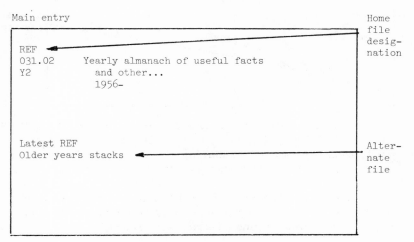

REF
031.02   Yearly almanach of useful facts
Y2   and other...
                 1956-

Latest REF   Alter-
Older years stacks   nate
                                                          file

Here is the shelf list card for the home file:

Shelf list entry

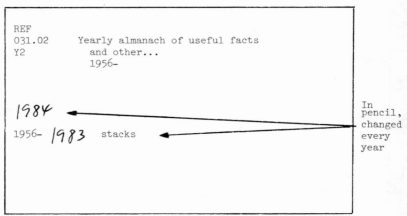

A dummy shelf list card is made for the alternate file:

Second shelf list entry

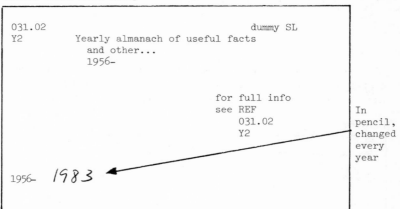

If a file splitter or straddler is ever removed from the library's holdings, it goes without saying that all shelf list cards must be removed, including the dummies. If that step is forgotten a blind reference is left in the shelf list.

A note on tracings: Since shelf list entries are manda-tory, it is not necessary to leave any tracings on the main entry. Only public added entries are traced.

Chapter 12

CROSS-REFERENCES _____

Even the most experienced library user cannot remember all
the headings under which relevant entries are filed in the
catalog. Not even a veteran cataloger can memorize all the
decisions that have been made in the past concerning the forms
of names and headings used or not used. To keep the catalog
at its highest level of usefulness for readers and librarians
alike, a coherent system of cross-references is maintained.

Cross-references are of two kinds. There are special
references from and to clearly defined terms, and there are
general references to classes of terms not specifically detailed.

Special cross-references are further divided into two
distinctly different types. A cross-reference either refers
the reader from a term not used in the catalog to one used.
This is the

See reference

or from a term used in the catalog to one or more terms that
are also used, which is the so-called

See also reference

The words "see" and "see also" are commonly underlined (or
printed in italics) to indicate that they are not part of the
cross-referenced terms.

SEE REFERENCES

See references are used to guide readers to alternate

forms of author's names and to alternate categorical headings.
They can be made from any unused term the cataloger chooses
to the appropriate term that is used as a heading in the catalog.   Most subject see references, however, will be made at
the suggestion of the published list of headings that has been
adopted.   In the Sears List of Subject Headings such sugges-
tions take this form: Names, Fictitious See Pseudonyms.
Here are some examples.   First, two author cross-references,
laid out in block format for easier typing.

```
        Clemens, Samuel Langhorne
        see
        Twain, Mark
```

```
        Lawick-Goodall, Jane, Barones van
        see
        Van Lawick-Goodall, Jane
```

Here are two subject cross-references:

```
        NEGRO HISTORY
        see
        AFRO-AMERICANS--HISTORY
```

```
        PORTER, WILLIAM SIDNEY
        see
        HENRY, O.
```

The INSPEC Thesaurus and many other similar specialized
lists of headings employ USE references instead of see references: Diesel engines   USE   Internal combustion engines.
For the card catalog this suggestion translates into:

> DIESEL ENGINES
> see
> INTERNAL COMBUSTION ENGINES

The see reference takes the reader from one heading
to one equivalent or approximately equivalent heading. Logically, then, the see reference is a 1:1 (one-to-one) reference.
It is a reference that leads from one term (Clemens, Samuel
Langhorne) to one other term (Twain, Mark). Catalogers who
follow established lists of subject headings will occasionally
find this logic defeated. In the Sears List, for example,
many of the suggested see references lead to more than one
term. An example is the following:

> Welfare state.   See Economic policy; Public welfare;
>   State, The

It is not clear from such a reference to which term one should
turn. Is "Economic policy" the equivalent of "Welfare state"?
Or is it part of the problem, or maybe the solution? It would
be clearer if the 1:1 principle were adhered to, A see B,
followed as necessary by B see also C, D, etc. Here is the
"Welfare state" example restructured:

```
        WELFARE STATE
        see
        PUBLIC WELFARE
```

This gives the catalog user a precise instruction on where to look. Under Public welfare, Economic policy can be mentioned in a see also reference:

```
                    PUBLIC WELFARE
                    see also
                    ECONOMIC POLICY
```

Under Economic policy, finally, other references might lead to relevant terms such as ECONOMIC ASSISTANCE or SOCIAL POLICY.

SEE ALSO REFERENCES

See also references are used to guide readers from a heading that is in use to one or more other headings that are also in use and may be helpful. See also references are made as needed at the suggestion of the published list of headings adopted. The Sears List, in the example shown in chapter 9, suggested: Tombs See also Brasses; Catacombs; Cemeteries; etc. If the library has one or more books under the heading TOMBS, one or more others under the heading CEMETERIES, but nothing under the headings BRASSES or CATACOMBS, then the cataloger will make one of the suggested cross-references:

> TOMBS
> see also
> CEMETERIES

Obviously, see also references do not attempt to guide readers to equivalent headings, only to related ones. Consequently, see also references can lead from a wider term to a narrower one or from a narrower term to a wider one, or they can connect terms that are on the same level of extension.

In specialized lists of terms, such as INSPEC Thesaurus, cross-reference directions often replace see also with abbreviations, such as BT for "broader term," RT for "related term," and so on: Internal combustion engines BT Engines RT Ignition.   In the card catalog this translates to

   INTERNAL COMBUSTION ENGINES
   see also
   ENGINES
   IGNITION

assuming, of course, that the library has material under all three headings. A case could be made for making such references even if nothing was under INTERNAL COMBUSTION ENGINES, on the theory that a see also reference is better than nothing.

Here are a few other examples of see also references. This one goes from a general to a specific heading, which is the most common direction:

```
        PHILOSOPHY
        see also
        ONTOLOGY
```

The next one goes from a narrow, specific term to a broad, general term, which is possible but not common:

```
VACUUM TUBES
see also
ELECTRONICS
```

Here is a see also reference between two terms that are on the same level:

```
TROUBADOURS
see also
TROUVERES
```

The reader is not compelled to follow a see also reference. The see also reference is merely a helpful suggestion. It can be from one term used in the catalog to one or more terms also used. This last condition, also used, is essential because nothing is more annoying than a reference to a term that is not there.

GENERAL REFERENCES

Occasionally, general references are made. They use any suitable free text instead of the formalized see also structure. Here is an example:

```
ABORTION

For pamphlets, brochures, and
similar uncataloged material
on this topic consult the
pamphlet file
```

The table on page 126 presents an overview of the various types of cross-references that occur in library catalogs.

CONTROLS

Whenever the term to which a cross-reference refers is withdrawn from the catalog, the cross-reference must also be withdrawn or a blind reference will be left in the catalog. Unfortunately, no cataloger can remember all the cross-references that are made. The librarian must therefore rely on a control system as a memory aid. In the case of subject references, the kind that is used most frequently, such a control system can be in the form of notes penciled right into the list of subject headings adopted by the library. Some libraries use lists that leave every other column blank for just this purpose.

Here is a see reference from the Sears List: Toadstools see Mushrooms. Here is the Sears List entry for Mushrooms:

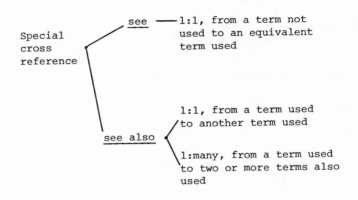

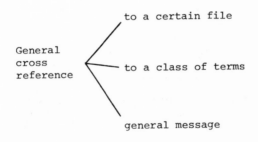

Mushrooms 589.2
See also Fungi
x   Toadstools
xx Fungi

The line marked "x" is a "control." The symbol "x" means
that a see reference was made from Toadstools to Mushrooms.
If the library has books under MUSHROOMS, the cataloger
might follow the suggestion and add this cross-reference on
page 127 to the catalog:

```
TOADSTOOLS
see
MUSHROOMS
```

If that is done, then the following control markings should
be made in the Sears List, in pencil for easier erasing:

Mushrooms   589.2
    See also Fungi
    x   ⌊Toadstools
    xx   Fungi

    .
    .
    .

⌊Toadstools   See   Mushrooms

        If it should happen later that the last book on mush-
rooms is withdrawn, a blind reference would be left. To prevent that, the cataloger, on withdrawing the last card with
the subject heading MUSHROOMS, looks up the term "Mushrooms" in the Sears List and finds the penciled control mark
under "x Toadstools." This reminds the cataloger to go back
to the catalog and pull the cross-reference from Toadstools
to Mushrooms. All that remains to be done now is to erase
the control marks in the book under Mushrooms and under
Toadstools.

        Of course, the moment a new edition of the Sears List
is published and adopted by the library all those penciled

control marks are lost unless they are faithfully transferred
to the new book, a tedious job subject to human error. An
alternate way to control cross-references is to maintain a control file on cards.

        A simple control file can be designed as follows. Any
cross-reference goes from something to something. On a cross-
reference card, the card that is filed in the public catalog
card, the term on top can be called the FROM term. The
term below is the TO term. A control card, then, is the ob-
verse of the cross reference card: it shows the TO term on
top and the FROM term below. The FROM term is marked
with the already familiar symbols that indicate type of reference (x = see from; xx = see also from). Here is a cross-
reference with its control card:

```
┌──────────────────────────────────────────────────────┐
│                                                        │
│                                                        │
│                                                        │
│              PHILOSOPHY                                │
│              see also                                  │
│              ONTOLOGY                                  │
│                                                        │
│                                                        │
├──────────────────────────────────────────────────────┤
│                                                        │
│                                                        │
│              ONTOLOGY                                  │
│         xx PHILOSOPHY                                  │
│                                                        │
│                                                        │
│                                                        │
│                                                        │
│                                                        │
│                                                        │
│                                                        │
│                                                        │
└──────────────────────────────────────────────────────┘
```

        The control card tells the cataloger that a see also
reference was made from PHILOSOPHY to ONTOLOGY. On the
following page is the control card for the Mark Twain reference from page 120:

```
        Twain, Mark
    x Clemens, Samuel Langhorne
```

It tells the cataloger that a <u>see</u> reference was made from
Clemens to Twain.

While the cross-reference cards in the public catalog
are filed by the FROM term, the control cards are filed by
the TO term in the same place where the shelf list is kept.

Should it happen that a cross-reference goes from one
term to several terms, such as in this example:

```
        PERSPECTIVE
        see also
        DRAWING
        PROJECTION
```

control cards are made for <u>each</u> TO term:

```
DRAWING
xx PERSPECTIVE
```

```
PROJECTION
xx PERSPECTIVE
```

What would happen if the term PROJECTION were abol-
ished? The removed heading is checked against the control
file. The previous control card shown above tells that a <u>see</u>
<u>also</u> reference exists from PERSPECTIVE to PROJECTION.
No one could possibly have remembered this without the aid
of the control file. The term PROJECTION on the cross-
reference card is now crossed out and the PROJECTION control card is removed from the control file. Here is what is
left:

In the
public
catalog

```
PERSPECTIVE
see also
DRAWING
PROJECTION
```

In the
control
file

```
                    DRAWING
                 xx PERSPECTIVE
```

Important: blind references may result if the control
file is not checked each time the last card for a heading is
removed from the catalog.

Occasionally, general references have to be inserted
into the catalog to guide readers. There is no standard
format for general references. Libraries use them in two ways.
One kind consists of a few explanatory words guiding readers
from a term to a certain special file of materials. The general
reference for ABORTION on page 125 is one example. Such
general references need not be controlled. When the last
pamphlet on abortion is discarded, the public catalog is
checked. The general reference filed under ABORTION is
simply removed from the catalog.

Sometimes general references are used to guide readers
from one term to a whole class of others. Here is an example
on page 132.

```
              QUOTATIONS, MAXIMS, ETC.

              Relevant material may be found under
              certain subjects, e.g.
              MUSIC__QUOTATIONS, MAXIMS, ETC.
```

The control card for this general reference looks like this:

```
              MUSIC--QUOTATIONS, MAXIMS, ETC.
        gen.  QUOTATIONS, MAXIMS, ETC.
```

If the subject heading MUSIC--QUOTATIONS, MAXIMS, ETC.
is removed from the catalog, the control file will warn the
cataloger to either remove the general reference from the
catalog or to change the example on it.

One thing that often mystifies library personnel long
after they think they have understood the mechanism of cross-
references and controls is the distinction between "see also"
and "xx." The explanation, therefore, bears repeating. If

any published list of subject headings shows an entry like this:

> Tornadoes
> See also   Cyclones; Storms
> xx   Storms; Winds

this means that three see also references are suggested. They are

```
        TORNADOES
        see also
        CYCLONES
        STORMS
```

```
        STORMS
        see also
        TORNADOES
```

```
        WINDS
        see also
        TORNADOES
```

The reader should notice that no references are suggested from Tornadoes to Winds and from Cyclones to Tornadoes.

Chapter 13

FILING _____

For the card catalog to be useful, the entries in it must be
arranged in a systematic way. It is often said that catalog
cards are filed alphabetically. This is an oversimplification.
In reality there are three different ordering principles that
apply from case to case. Certainly, many entries are filed
alphabetically,

> Some selected...
> Two for tea...
> Under elm trees...

in other words, S,T,U. But others are filed numerically,

> 3 Musketeers...
> 4 in a ...
> 5 famous plays...

and some are filed by context,

> Athenaeum of Philadelphia
> Guide to museum...
>
> ATHENAEUM OF PHILADELPHIA
> Beginnings of the American...

i.e., the corporate author before the subject of the same name,
regardless of the alphabetical order of the words that follow.

The basic principle underlying all three examples is that
a correctly filed entry follows an entry of lower rank and is

followed by an entry of higher rank. How to determine the
rank of entries has been codified in a book, <u>ALA Filing Rules</u>
(American Library Association, Chicago, 1980). These newest
guidelines are now widely accepted as standard in American
libraries. They are followed here in principle with minor
changes.

In the past, it was often said that filing meant putting
"words" in order. <u>ALA Filing Rules</u> recognize a broader concept, replacing "word" by what is known as "character
string."

A character is any graphic symbol used as a unit in
writing or printing. The letter A, for example, is an alphabetical character. The numeral 3 is a numeric character.
The sign $ is another type of character. Any single charac-
ter, and any group of two or more characters that stand together, forms a character string. Thus, a word is a character string. But notice: not all character strings are words.

There are two kinds of character strings, alphabetic
strings and numeric strings.

ALPHABETIC FILING

An alphabetic character string can be defined as a
letter or group of letters or other nonnumeric characters set
off by numeric characters, spaces, dashes, hyphens, diagonal
slashes, or periods (the six alphabetic string delimiters).
Here are some examples of alphabetic character strings:

BIOLOGY

This is a purely alphabetic string, seven alphabetic characters
surrounded by spaces.

ART--HISTORY

Both of these strings are delimited by a space on one side
and a dash on the other (since the typewriter does not have
a dash two hyphens are customarily used to simulate it).

Lloyd-Jones

These two strings are delimited by a space on one side and a hyphen on the other.

        and/or

These are two strings because they have a space on one side and a diagonal slash on the other.

        Selected works.

The word "works" is a string because it starts with a space and ends with a period.

        Boy's

This is one alphabetic character string, too. It consists of four letters and one non-numeric character set off by spaces. Notice that the apostrophe is not a string delimiter but is a symbol that is ignored, where "ignored" means that it is treated as if it were not there, not as if it were a space. For filing purposes, thus, the following three strings are equivalent: boys, boy's, and boys'.

        3M

Here the letter M is one character string. It is delimited on the left by the numeric character 3 and on the right by a space. By the same token, 3 is a numeric string, but more about numeric strings below.

        Alphabetic strings are filed in the customary order of the English alphabet. In reality, of course, so-called alpha-betical filing is nothing but a special case of numerical filing. For when we arrange the letters of the English alphabet in their alphabetical order we actually map them mentally, one for one, to the sequence of integers from +1 to +26. Here is a table that shows how we map them:

A 1	H 8	O 15	U 21
B 2	I 9	P 16	V 22
C 3	J 10	Q 17	W 23
D 4	K 11	R 18	X 24
E 5	L 12	S 19	Y 25
F 6	M 13	T 20	Z 26
G 7	N 14		

After mapping the letters to their numerical equivalents we
can put them in rank order. Thus, when we file B behind A
we do so because B = 2, A = 1, and 1 is less than 2. In
other words, we file B behind A because B outranks A, has a
higher numerical value.

Often two compared alphabetic strings begin with different letters. Rank order is then determined on the basis of
the difference in the first letter (Abel is less than Baker).

Sometimes strings begin with the same letters. The rank
difference is then determined by a subsequent letter pair.
Here is an example:

> Abel
> Abraham

The difference here comes in the third letter pair, e vs. r.
Since e = 5, r = 18, and 5 is less than 18, we file Abel before
Abraham.

Occasionally two compared strings correspond in symbol
content to the very end of one of them. Here is an example:

> Abel
> Abelson

Rank difference here comes in the fifth letter pair. After the
fourth letter in "Abel" is "nothing." After the fourth letter
in "Abelson" is "s." "Nothing," of course, is mapped to the
number 0; "s," to 19. And since 0 is less than 19, Abelson
outranks Abel. In the ALA Filing Rules the phenomenon of
the zero-valued space is given the picturesque name of the
"nothing before something" rule.

Often two compared entries begin with the same string.
Filing then proceeds by the next string as in this example:

> Mass media in...
> Mass violence in...

It is important to note that library filing is string by
string:

> Beaver dam
> Beaver Falls
> Beaverbrook

and not character by character as, for example, in <u>Collier's</u>
<u>Encyclopedia</u>:

> Beaverbrook
> Beaver dam
> Beaver Falls

   Different persons occasionally have identical names.
Filing then is by given names:

> Frederick, John
> Frederick, Justus

   Occasionally, two persons have exactly the same name.
Filing is then by date:

> Vianna, Oduvaldo, 1892-1972
> Vianna, Oduvaldo, 1936-1974

   As the catalog grows in size, different books by the
same author will appear. Since in such cases the author headings are identical, filing proceeds by the title:

> Frost, Robert
> Boy's will ...

> Frost, Robert
> In the clearing ...

   The same thing happens when two books are cataloged
under identical subject headings:

> TEACHING
> Humanism in the ...

> TEACHING
> Retreat from learning ...

   One important principle of the <u>ALA Filing Rules</u> is that
alphabetic characters are considered in exactly the form and
order in which they appear in the string. This principle
emphasizes how character strings look rather than how they
sound or what they mean.

Here are some of the fine points of alphabetic filing
(the rule numbers refer to the <u>ALA Filing Rules</u> of 1980):

Mc vs. Mac (Rules 1 and 2.1)

Filers familiar with the old ALA rules of 1968 remember
that McFarland was filed as if it were spelled MacFarland.
This is no longer done. All alphabetic strings are filed as
spelled, not as pronounced. Thus, the following three words
are in correct order:

> MacGower
> Machinery
> McFarland

Modified Letters (Rule 1.1)

Modified letters are treated like their unmodified counter-
parts. The German ä is considered equivalent to the English
a. The Polish slashed *ł* is equated with the simple l. Also,
the ligature œ is considered to be equal to the letter o followed by the letter e; the Spanish digraph ll is considered to
be an l followed by another l; and so forth. The following
names are in correct order:

> Oberg
> Oster
> Østerling
> Ostrowsky
> Ulloa
> Ulmer

Note that some libraries will file the German ä as if spelled
ae, ö as if spelled oe, and so on. Spanish librarians will
file the digraph ll after the plain l.

Letters of non-Latin alphabets such as Greek Ψ, must
be transliterated. Thus Ψ becomes psi. The component
letters are then mapped to 16, 19, and 9, respectively. After
this, the Greek letter can be filed,

> PARTNERSHIP
> Ψ FACTOR (i.e., PSI FACTOR)
> PSYCHOLOGY

Non-alphabetic non-numeric signs and symbols (Rule 1.2)

In alphabetic strings all non-alphabetic symbols that are
neither numeric symbols nor other string delimiters (i.e.,
not dash, hyphen, slash, or period) are ignored, where ignored means treated as if it did not exist, not as if it were
a space. Thus K*A*P*L*A*N is filed as KAPLAN. Warning:
letters, signs, and symbols in numeric strings follow different
rules.

Numeric symbols next to alphabetic characters (Rule 8.6)

If a numeric symbol stands next to an alphabetic string,
it is considered a string delimiter and is not considered to be
part of the adjacent alphabetic string. The following three
lines are in correct order:

H_2O (i.e., the alphabetic string H followed by the
numeric string 2)

H and H

Horvath

It should be noted that, all else being equal, numbers file
before letters, "H 2" before "H and."

Ampersand (Rule 1.3)

The most practical way to deal with the ampersand sign
(&) is probably the "with" option of Rule 1.3. Under that
option, the symbol & is filed as if it were spelled out in the
language in question. The following entries are in order:

A & O International (& = and, English)
A and P Company
A & B Internationale (& = et, French)
A un joven
A & O im Ganzen (& = und, German)
A une dame

Abbreviations (Rule 3)

Abbreviations that are not relators or terms of honor
and address (see below, page 143) are arranged exactly
as written. Thus, "Mr." files as the string MR between "Misty" and "Muzhik," in other words not as if spelled
Mister. The following data elements are in correct filing
order:

Mississippi
Mister Roberts
Mr. Adams
Ms. Adams

Initial articles (Rule 4)
 If the advice given on page 53 is followed, namely to
suppress all leading articles in the nominative case, then Rule
4, which directs filers to ignore such articles, becomes super-
fluous as a filing rule. But the cataloger must still apply the
same principles in building headings, and bibliographic descriptions and must be careful to distinguish among cases and
between articles, numerals, and pronouns. The rule applies
to all languages, which is hard to do for persons with limited
linguistic background. Here are some examples:

The Black Hole becomes Black Hole
Ein Ding zum Lachen becomes Ding
 zum Lachen
Los jovenes de mañana becomes
 Jovenes de mañana

"The," "Ein," and "Los," are articles in the nominative case.
But compare these examples:

Ein Ding weiss ich gewiss
Los de abajo

These file under "Ein" and "Los," respectively, because "ein"
is a numeral or possibly an article in the accusative case, and
"los" is a pronoun! Many catalogers and catalog users may
find it too difficult to distinguish between articles and other
types of words of this nature. A compromise is possible:
drop all English initial articles (a, an, the) and leave all non-
English words in place. Here is the same example in compromise order:

Black Hole
Ein Ding weiss ich gewiss
Ein Ding zum Lachen
Los de Abajo
Los jovenes de manana

Initial articles that are part of a personal name
 Articles at the beginning of proper names are treated
as prefixes according to Rule 6.

Articles between words
      Articles that appear inside a title or heading, i.e., not
in the initial or leading position, are filed like other strings:

            Will a unicorn...
            Will and power
            Will the hustler
            Will they conquer...
            Williamsburg

Initials (Rule 5)
      Initials are single letter abbreviations of words or
names. They are treated as single letter strings:

            Greasepaint
            I am a camera
            I. and his friend J.
            I built a bridge
            Iambic pentameters

Initialisms and acronyms (Rule 5)
      Initialisms, acronyms, and other abbreviations consisting
of two or more characters enclosed by string delimiters (i.e.,
numerical characters, spaces, dashes, hyphens, slashes, and
periods) are treated as alphabetic strings or "words":

            I must go now
            I.N.T.E.L.S.A.T. (I-space-N-space etc.)
            Iberian Peninsula
            IBM Applications Program
            If this be error

Prefixes (Rule 6)
      Prefixes in proper names that are separated from the
rest of the name by a space or a hyphen are treated as separate strings. Prefixes connected with the name by an apostrophe are considered part of the name:

            Damask
            D'Arcy, John (i.e., DARCY)
            De Forest, Angela
            Death comes
            Defoe
            Lobo-Zarra, Arturo
            Lobos

>   Los Angeles
>   Losable and lost

Double names (Rule 3)

Double names such as "Watts-Dunton, Theodore" or "Lloyd George, David" are treated according to the regular rules for alphabetic strings,

>   Lloyd, Emma
>   Lloyd George, David
>   Lloyd, Sarah
>   .
>   .
>   .
>   Watts, Beulah
>   Watts-Dunton, Theodore
>   Watts, George

Relators (Rule 9)

Abbreviations such as "ed." or "comp." following an author's name are called relators or function designators. They are disregarded in filing.

Terms of honor (Rule 10)

Terms of honor and address added to names in author and subject headings, such as "Lord," "Sir," "Dr.," "Mr.," are disregarded:

>   John, Dr. Ambrose
>   John, Charles
>   John, Nancy
>   John, Mrs. William

NUMERIC FILING

Numeric strings have their own rules. A numeric string can be defined as any Arabic or Roman numeral or group of numeric characters, with or without punctuation marks and alphabetical auxiliaries, that together express one cardinal or ordinal number. Here are ten numeric strings (not in any order):

>   5
>   5th

5^e (French ordinal, equals 5th)
5. (German ordinal, equals 5th)
V
15
XV
1/5 (a fraction, equals .2)
.2 (a decimal fraction, equals 1/5)
2 4/5 (a mixed number, equals 2.8)

According to Rule 1 all numeric strings file before alphabetic strings.

200 years
1001 nights
Abendstern
Best
The year 2000
The year after

When ranked among themselves, numeric strings, cardinal and ordinal numbers being treated alike, are filed in ascending numerical order (Rule 8).

Numerical strings placed next to non-numerical characters which do not have numerical significance are considered to be separated from these non-numerical characters:

2G Model 6 (filed as 2 G)

2^e partie (2^e, French equivalent of 2nd, is filed as 2)

.

.

200 Notions
200T Model ...
200 Uncommon...

As shown in the example above, non-numerical characters which do have numerical significance in numerical strings are considered part of the numerical strings.

One fine point of numerical filing was left unsettled by the ALA Filing Rules of 1980, the rank order of fractions. It is recommended here that all fractions are filed by their numerical values. Here is a comprehensive example:

.5 and the...
1/2 by a... (.5 and $\frac{1}{2}$ are equivalent)
2 4/5
3.1416
V_e and more
5^e arrondissement
5 can be
5th column
5. Mann
15 and then
XV could go
17th Army
17^e Couronne
200
5,000.3 (i.e. 5 thousand and 3/10)
Abendstern
Borgman, Hans, 1903-
Borgman, Hans, 1941-

Numbers that appear inside a heading rather than at the beginning are also subarranged numerically:

LOUIS II
LOUIS III
LOUIS IV, DUKE OF...
LOUIS IV, KING OF
MARINE BIOLOGY
Mental Health, 6th Conference
Mental Health, 7th Conference
Mental health and...

Ranges of dates with unequal starting points are arranged in ascending numerical order by starting points:

GREAT BRITAIN--HISTORY--1660-1714
GREAT BRITAIN--HISTORY--1689-1714

Ranges of dates with identical starting points are arranged in ascending numerical order by their endpoints:

GREAT BRITAIN--POLITICS AND GOVERNMENT
--1485-1509
GREAT BRITAIN--POLITICS AND GOVERNMENT
--1485-1603

If a single number or open range and a closed range with identical starting point are to be compared, the single number files first:

> ...HISTORY--1900-
> ...HISTORY--1900-1914

If numbers are spelled out they are filed alphabetically, not numerically:

> Twenty years
> Two men

CONTEXTUAL FILING

When two compared entries differ in access points, filing is based on simple alphabetical or numerical rank order.

When two compared entries have equivalent headings, as in this example,

> Nash, Ogden
> Old dog barks...
>
> Nash, Ogden
> You can't get...

filing proceeds by the next element that is different, in this case "Old" before "You." In this case the headings were equal in symbol content as well as in function: they were both author headings. But occasionally it happens that two compared entries have headings that are equivalent in symbol content, but one is an author heading, the other is a subject heading:

> Aristotle
> Republic and other ...
>
> ARISTOTLE
> Life of Aristotle ...

Two entries of this kind are filed, not alphabetically (Life before Republic) but according to function or context (Aristotle as author before Aristotle as subject).

Of course, when author and title entries are interfiled, the arrangement is straightforward and function is ignored:

Frost damage on citrus...

Frost in perspective

Frost, Robert
Selected works by ...

Frost und sein Kreis...

Also, when different subject headings beginning with the same word are interfiled, arrangement is straightforward:

WASHINGTON CALENDAR
WASHINGTON, GEORGE
WASHINGTON POST

Undivided subject headings are filed before divided subject headings beginning with the same main heading:

JEWS
History of seven...

JEWS--BIOGRAPHY
Five masters of the...

SUBARRANGEMENT

If two or more items have the same title, the <u>ALA Filing Rules</u> specifies subarrangement by date (Rule 2.3):

Business law / by Carl Hinze. -- New York : Globe, 1978.

Business law / by Joe Doe. -- Chicago : Hopner, 1980.

Business law / by Carl Hinze. -- 2nd ed. -- New York : Globe, 1981.

The same rule applies when two compared subject entries have identical headings and identical titles:

PHILOSOPHY
What is philosophy? / by Marie White. -- New York: Domby, 1970.

PHILOSOPHY
What is philosophy? / by John Brown. -- Boston :
Harms, 1980.

It may be easier for all concerned to subarrange such
entries alphabetically by authors' last names:

Business law / by Joe Doe ...

Business law / by Carl Hinze ... 1978.

Business law / by Carl Hinze ... 1981.

PHILOSOPHY
What is philosophy? / John Brown...

PHILOSOPHY
What is philosophy? / by Marie White ...

Some titles consist of only one part, the "title proper."
Filing of simple "titles proper" is straightforward:

Algebra / by Joe Doe. -- New York : Scherer, 1984.

Algebra and geometry / by Henry Fine. -- Glendale :
Gardner, 1982.

Some titles have subtitles. They consist of a title proper
and a subtitle. By the ALA filing rules only the title proper
is considered for filing. This can lead to very esoteric complications. An alternate rule is suggested here: consider all
that precedes the author statement to be the title:

Algebra / by Joe Doe. -- New York : Scherer, 1981.

Algebra and geometry / by Henry Fine. -- Glendale :
Gardner, 1982.

Algebra: Selected rules / ed. by Jane Sulk. --
Boston : Rausch, 1980

DIVIDED CATALOGS

The ALA Filing Rules of 1980 were designed for the so-
called "dictionary catalog," a catalog wherein author, title,
and categorical entries are arranged in one sequence. Some
libraries find it helpful to arrange their catalog in two divisions (author/title and subject) or to divide it into three

sequences (author, title, and subject). Filing into divided
catalogs is simpler. Since all categorical added entries are
filed separately, the question of context does not come up.

FILING OF CROSS-REFERENCES

See references are filed by the same rules that apply
to other entries. For see also references a special rule ap-
plies--they are filed ahead of their corresponding catalog entries:

JEWS
see also
ISRAELIS

JEWS
History of seven ...

JEWS--BIOGRAPHY
Five masters of the ...

JOBBERS
see
WHOLESALERS

LOCATION CODE OR "CALL NUMBER"
FILING

The filing of books or shelf list cards by location codes
is done as follows. The first step is to determine the file
designation. A shelf list card marked "840 A2," for example,
indicates by the absence of a special file designation that it
belongs into the "stack" shelf list, the list of all books that
reside in the regular book stacks. If the card were marked
"REF 840 A2" instead, it would have to be filed in the "reference" shelf list. If marked "Oversize 840 A2" it would go
into the "oversize" shelf list, and so on.

The second step in location code filing is the ordering
by notation. This step varies somewhat depending on the
classification or shelf location system used. Only the two
major classification systems are considered here.

Dewey Number Filing

If the Dewey system is used, location code filing is first a question of numerical order. Here are two shelf list cards in order:

> 840
> B9
>
> 845
> A2

Decimal fractions, too, are filed numerically:

> 845.1
> P6
>
> 845.2
> M2

If the class symbols are alike in two compared codes, filing proceeds by the book symbols:

> 840
> A6
>
> 840
> B4

Should the compared book symbols begin with the same letters, filing is by the numerical part:

> 840
> B3
>
> 840
> B4

It should be noted that numbers in book symbols are considered decimals, not integers. The reason, of course, is that book symbols must be expandable to preserve the alphabetical order of the titles they represent, which can often only be achieved by interpolating a fraction between integers. This means that the numerical parts of two compared book symbols are evaluated as if they were preceded by decimal points. Here is an example:

840
H3

840
H35

840
H4

The decimal .35 is less than the decimal .4, which is why
H35 comes before H4, as shown.

Here is a comprehensive example with Dewey numbers:

840
A6

840
B3

840
B4

840
B9

840
H35

840
H4

845
A2

845
A2
B6

845.1
P6

845.2
M2

Library of Congress Symbol Filing

If the Library of Congress classification system, a mixed
notation of alphabetical and numerical symbols, is used, filing
is first a question of alphabetical order:

QD
11
S29

QE
6
A22

If the alphabetical symbols are equal in two compared codes, filing is by the numerical part of the notation:

Q
6
Z7

Q
11
A2

If the numerical part includes a decimal fraction, filing is still by numerical magnitude:

Q
10.8
T6

Q
11
S2

If the letters and numbers in the first two lines of a Library of Congress location code are alike, filing proceeds by the next part, which is almost always alphanumeric:

QD
11
R3

QD
11
S2

If the letters of that part of the code are alike, filing is by the numerical part, read as decimals:

QD
11
S29 (i.e., .29)

```
QD
11
S3 (i.e., .3)
```

A comprehensive example with Library of Congress codes follows.

```
Q                          QD
6                          11
Z7                         S29

Q                          QD
10.8                       11
T6                         S3

Q                          QE
11                         6
A2                         A22

Q                          QE
11                         6
S2                         A22
                           F5
QD
11                         QE
R3                         6
                           A3
QD
11
S2
```

Appendix A

EXAMPLES _____

On the following pages are thirteen examples of catalog cards
for different types of items. The type numbers refer to the
chart on page 6.

EXAMPLE 1

A stand-alone work of type 1, one personal author.

Main entry

```
635
G2          Gardening by the foot : mini grow-boxes
               for maxi yields / [by] Jacob R. Mitt-
               leider. -- Bountiful, UT : Horizon
               Publishers, 1981.
            143 p.


1. VEGETABLE GARDENING.   2. CONTAINER GARDENING.
I. Mittleider, Jacob R.   II. Title: Mini grow-
boxes for maxi yields.
```

First subject added entry

```
635              VEGETABLE GARDENING
G2          Gardening by the foot : mini grow-boxes
               for maxi yields / [by] Jacob R. Mitt-
               leider. -- Bountiful, UT :Horizon
               Publishers, 1981.
            143 p.
```

EXAMPLE 1 (cont.)

Second subject added entry

```
635              CONTAINER GARDENING
G2               Gardening by the foot : mini grow-boxes
                 for maxi yields / [by] Jacob R. Mitt-
                 leider. -- Bountiful, UT : Horizon
                 Publishers, 1981.
                 143 p.
```

Author added entry

```
635              Mittleider, Jacob R.
G2               Gardening by the foot : mini grow-boxes
                 for maxi yields / [by] Jacob R. Mitt-
                 leider. -- Bountiful, UT : Horizon
                 Publishers, 1981.
                 143 p.
```

EXAMPLE 1 (cont.)

Title added entry

```
635              Mini grow-boxes for maxi yields
G2               Gardening by the foot : mini grow-boxes
                   for maxi yields / [by] Jacob R. Mitt-
                   leider. -- Bountiful, UT : Horizon
                   Publishers, 1981.
                 143 p.
```

Shelf list card

```
635
G2               Gardening by the foot : mini grow-boxes
                   for maxi yields / [by] Jacob R. Mitt-
                   leider. -- Bountiful, UT : Horizon
                   Publishers, 1981.
                 143 p.


(space for housekeeping information...)
```

EXAMPLE 2

A stand-alone work of type 1, two personal authors.

Main entry

```
692.1
R3          Reading construction drawings / Paul I.
            Wallach ; Donald E. Hepler. -- New
            York : McGraw-Hill, 1981.
            313 p.




    1. SPECIFICATION WRITING.   2. BUILDING--CONTRACTS AND
    SPECIFICATIONS. I. Wallach, Paul I. II. Hepler, Donald E.
```

First subject added entry

```
692.1       SPECIFICATION WRITING
R3          Reading construction drawings / Paul I.
            Wallach ; Donald E. Hepler. -- New
            York : McGraw-Hill, 1981.
            313 p.
```

EXAMPLE 2 (cont.)

Second subject added entry

```
692.1           BUILDING--CONTRACTS AND SPECIFICATIONS
R3              Reading construction drawings / Paul I.
                Wallach ; Donald E. Hepler. -- New
                York : McGraw-Hill, 1981.
                313 p.
```

First author added entry

```
692.1           Wallach, Paul I.
R3              Reading construction drawings / Paul I.
                Wallach ; Donald E. Hepler. -- New
                York : McGraw-Hill, 1981.
                313 p.
```

EXAMPLE 2 (cont.)

Second author added entry

```
692.1          Hepler, Donald E.
R3             Reading construction drawings / Paul I.
               Wallach ; Donald E. Hepler. -- New
               York : McGraw-Hill, 1981.
               313 p.
```

Shelf list card

```
692.1
R3             Reading construction drawings / Paul I.
               Wallach ; Donald E. Hepler. -- New
               York : McGraw-Hill, 1981.
               313 p.



(space for housekeeping information)
```

EXAMPLE 3

A stand-alone work of type 1, one corporate author and several personal authors.

Main entry

```
624.2
G9          Guide for the field testing of bridges /
            prepared by the Working Committee on
            Safety ; B. Bakht [et al.]. -- New
            York : American Society of Civil
            Engineers, 1980.
            72 p.


1. BRIDGES--TESTING.   I. American Society of Civil
Engineers. Working Committee on Safety.   II. Bakht, B.
```

Subject added entry

```
624.2          BRIDGES--TESTING
G9          Guide for the field testing of bridges /
            prepared by the Working Committee on
            Safety ; B. Bakht [et al.]. -- New
            York : American Society of Civil
            Engineers, 1980.
            72 p.
```

EXAMPLE 3 (cont.)

First author added entry

```
624.2       American Society of Civil Engineers.
G9          Working Committee on Safety
            Guide for the field testing of bridges /
            prepared by the Working Committee on
            Safety ; B. Bakht [et al.]. -- New
            York : American Society of Civil
            Engineers, 1980.
            72 p.
```


Second author added entry

```
624.2       Bakht, B.
G9          Guide for the field testing of bridges /
            prepared by the Working Committee on
            Safety ; B. Bakht [et al.]. -- New
            York : American Society of Civil
            Engineers, 1980.
            72 p.
```

EXAMPLE 3 (cont.)

Shelf list card

```
624.2
G9          Guide for the field testing of bridges /
            prepared by the Working Committee on
            Safety ; B. Bakht [et al.]. -- New
            York : American Society of Civil
            Engineers, 1980
            72 p.


(space for housekeeping information...)
```

EXAMPLE 4

A one-volume collection of articles, a book of type 2; one
person named as editor.

Main entry

```
136.7354
A4          Adolescent : a book of readings / edited
            by Jerome M. Seidman. -- Rev. ed. --
            New York : Holt, 1960.
            870 p.




       1. ADOLESCENCE.  I. Seidman, Jerome M., ed.


```

Subject added entry

```
136.7354    ADOLESCENCE
A4          Adolescent : a book of readings / edited
            by Jerome M. Seidman. -- Rev. ed. --
            New York : Holt, 1960.
            870 p.
```

EXAMPLE 4 (cont.)

Author added entry

```
136.7354      Seidman, Jerome M., ed.
A4            Adolescent : a book of readings / edited
              by Jerome M. Seidman. -- Rev. ed. --
              New York : Holt, 1960.
              870 p.
```

Shelf list card

```
136.7354
A4            Adolescent : a book of readings / edited
             by Jerome M. Seidman. -- Rev. ed. --
             New York : Holt, 1960.
             870 p.



(space for housekeeping information)
```

EXAMPLE 5

A one-volume collection of papers presented at a meeting,
a book of type 2; two editors.

Main entry

574.19
P6   Photoreception and sensory transduction /
                edited by Francesco Lenci and Giuliano
                Colombetti. -- New York : Planor Press,
                1980.
                422 p.

                Papers presented at the Advanced Institute
                of Photoreception, Versilia, Italy, 1979.

1. PHOTORECEPTORS.   2. SENSES AND SENSATION.   I. Ad-
vanced Institute of Photoreception, Versilia, Italy,

1979. II.Lenci, Francesco. III. Colombetti,
Giuliano.

First subject added entry

574.19   PHOTORECEPTORS
P6   Photoreception and sensory transduction /
                edited by Francesco Lenci and Giuliano
                Colombetti. -- New York : Palnor Press,
                1980.
                422 p.

EXAMPLE 5 (cont.)

Second subject added entry

```
574.19          SENSES AND SENSATION
P6              Photoreception and sensory transduction /
                edited by Francesco Lenci and Giuliano
                Colombetti. -- New York : Planor Press,
                1980.
                422 p.
```

First author added entry

```
574.19          Advanced Institute of Photoreception,
P6              Versilia, Italy, 1979
                Photoreception and sensory transduction /
                edited by Francesco Lenci and Giuliano
                Colombetti. -- New York : Planor Press,
                1980.
                422 p.
```

EXAMPLE 5 (cont.)

Second author added entry

```
574.19        Lenci, Francesco
P6            Photoreception and sensory transduction /
                edited by Francesco Lenci and Giuliano
                Colombetti. -- New York : Planor Press,
                1980.
                422 p.
```

Third author added entry

```
574.19        Colombetti, Giuliano
P6            Photoreception and sensory transduction /
                edited by Francesco Lenci and Giuliano
                Colombetti. -- New York : Planor Press,
                1980.
                422 p.
```

EXAMPLE 5 (cont.)

Shelf list card

```
574.19
P6           Photoreception and sensory transduction /
                edited by Francesco Lenci and Giuliano
                Colombetti. -- New York : Planor Press,
                1980.
                422 p.


(space for housekeeping information...)
```

EXAMPLE 6

A one-document collection of recorded musical pieces, an item
of type 2; one person named as performer.

Main entry

```
AUDIO
              Virgil Fox playing the organ at the
                 Riverside Church. -- [New York] : RCA,
                 [1950]
              Sound disc : 33 1/3 rpm, mono. ; 12 in.

              RCA Victor LM 2268


I. Fox, Virgil.
```

Author (i.e., performer) added entry

```
AUDIO         Fox, Virgil
              Virgil Fox playing the organ at the
                 Riverside Church. -- [New York] : RCA,
                 [1950]
              Sound disc : 33 1/3 rpm, mono. ; 12 in.

              RCA Victor LM 2268
```

EXAMPLE 6 (cont.)

Shelf list card

```
AUDIO
            Virgil Fox playing the organ at the
            Riverside Church. -- [New York] : RCA,
            [1950]
            Sound disc : 33 1/3 rpm,mono. ; 12 in.




(space for housekeeping information...)

```

EXAMPLE 7

A special issue of a periodical which contains one work. An
item of type 3, cataloged under the document description
principle. One personal author.

Main entry

```
336.2
M5          Mineral severance taxes in Western States :
              economic considerations / Sandra Black-
              stone. -- Golden : Colorado School of
              Mines, 1981.
              39 p.

              Colorado School of Mines Quarterly, v. 75,
              num. 3, ISSN 0010-1753

1. MINES AND MINERAL RESOURCES--TAXATION--THE WEST
I. Blackstone, Sandra. II. Title: Colorado School
of Mines Quarterly, v. 75, num. 3, July 1980.
```

Subject added entry

```
336.2       MINES AND MINERAL RESOURCES--TAXATION
M5            --THE WEST
            Mineral severance taxes in Western States :
              economic considerations / Sandra Black-
              stone. -- Golden : Colorado School of
              Mines, 1981.
              39 p.
```

EXAMPLE 7 (cont.)

Author added entry

```
336.2        Blackstone, Sandra
M5           Mineral severance taxes in Western States :
             economic considerations / Sandra Black-
             stone. -- Golden : Colorado School of
             Mines, 1981.
             39 p.
```

Connective added entry (set title)

```
336.2        Colorado School of Mines Quarterly,
M5           v. 75, num. 3, July 1980.
             Mineral severance taxes in Western States :
             economic considerations / Sandra Black-
             stone. -- Golden : Colorado School of
             Mines, 1981.
             39 p.
```

EXAMPLE 7 (cont.)

Shelf list card

```
336.2
M5         Mineral severance taxes in Western States :
             economic considerations / Sandra Black-
             stone. -- Golden : Colorado School of
             Mines, 1981.
             39 p.



           (space for housekeeping information)
```

EXAMPLE 8

An issue of a periodical that has its own document title. An
item of type 6 cataloged under the document description principle. One editor.

Main entry

```
320.05
P7         Police and violence / special editor
           Lawrence W. Sherman. -- Philadelphia :
           American Academy of Political and
           Social Science, 1980.
           211 p.

           Annals of the American Academy of
           Political and Social Science, v. 452,
           ISSN 0002-7162

1. POLICE--UNITED STATES.  2. VIOLENCE--UNITED STATES.
I. Sherman, Lawrence W., ed.  II. Title: Annals of the
American Academy of Political and Social Science, v. 452.
```

First subject added entry

```
320.05     POLICE--UNITED STATES
P7         Police and violence / special editor
           Lawrence W. Sherman. -- Philadelphia :
           American Academy of Political and
           Social Science, 1980.
           211 p.
```

EXAMPLE 8 (cont.)

Second subject added entry

```
320.05          VIOLENCE--UNITED STATES
P7              Police and violence / special editor
                Lawrence W. Sherman. -- Philadelphia :
                American Academy of Political and
                Social Science, 1980.
                211 p.
```

Author added entry

```
320.05          Sherman, Lawrence W., ed.
P7              Police and violence / special editor
                Lawrence W. Sherman. -- Philadelphia :
                American Academy of Political and
                Social Science, 1980.
                211 p.
```

EXAMPLE 8 (cont.)

Connective added entry (set title)

```
320.05        Annals of the American Academy of Political
P7            and Social Science, v. 452
              Police and violence / special editor
              Lawrence W. Sherman. -- Philadelphia :
              American Academy of Political and
              Social Science, 1980.
              211 p.
```

Shelf list card

```
320.05
P7            Police and violence / special editor
              Lawrence W. Sherman. -- Philadelphia :
              American Academy of Political and
              Social Science, 1980.
              211 p.



(space for housekeeping information)
```

EXAMPLE 9

A periodical, an item of type 7. Housekeeping information
kept on a special periodical check-in-card; no shelf list.

Main entry

```
              Journal of earth. -- New York :
                American Earth Society, 1984-

                v. 1, num. 1-

                Quarterly




     I. American Earth Society.
```

Author added entry

```
                American Earth Society
              Journal of earth. -- New York :
                American Earth Society, 1984-

                v. 1, num. 1-
```

EXAMPLE 10

A two-volume work, a book of type 8; one editor.

Main entry

```
621.48
R4            Research, training, test, and production
              reactor directory / Reed Burn, editor ,
              S. Krapp, project manager. -- La Grange
              Park, IL : American Nuclear Society,
              1980.
              2 v. (1922 p.)




1. NUCLEAR REACTORS--UNITED STATES.   I. Burn, Reed.
II. American Nuclear Society.
```

Subject added entry

```
621.48        NUCLEAR REACTORS--UNITED STATES
R4            Research, training, test, and production
              reactor directory / Reed Burn, editor ;
              S. Krapp, project manager. -- La Grange
              Park, IL : American Nuclear Society,
              1980.
              2 v. (1922 p)
```

EXAMPLE 10 (cont.)

First author added entry

```
621.48        Burn, Reed
R4            Research, training, test, and production
              reactor directory / Reed Burn, editor ;
              S. Krapp, project manager. -- La Grange
              Park, IL : American Nuclear Society,
              1980.
              2 v. (1922 p.)
```

Second author added entry

```
621.48        American Nuclear Society
R4            Research, training, test, and production
              reactor directory / Reed Burn, editor ;
              S. Krapp, project manager. -- La Grange
              Park, IL ı American Nuclear Society,
              1980.
              2 v. (1922 p.)
```

EXAMPLE 10 (cont.)

Shelf list card

```
621.48
R4              Research, training, test, and production
                reactor directory / Reed Burn, editor ;
                S. Krapp, project manager. -- La Grange
                Park, IL : American Nuclear Society,
                1980.
                2 v. (1922 p.)


(space for housekeeping information)
```

EXAMPLE 11

An item of type 5 -- a set of books wherein each has its own
distinctive title. One of the three books of the set is here
cataloged under the document description principle. One work
analytic has been made for one of the essays contained in the
volume. Compare also with example 12.

Main entry

```
QE
39          Ocean floor / ed. by Hamdy Bolles. --
0 3             New York : Bagsby, 1980.
                540 p.

                The Oceans, v. 2




1. SUBMARINE GEOLOGY.  I. Bolles, Hamdy, ed.
II. Title: Oceans, v. 2.  II. Ewing, Thomas.  Structure
of the Gulf of Mexico, in

```

Subject added entry

```
QE          SUBMARINE GEOLOGY
39          Ocean floor / ed. by Hamdy Bolles. --
0 3             New York : Bagsby, 1980.
                540 p.

```

EXAMPLE 11 (cont.)

Author added entry

```
QE                Bolles, Hamdy, ed.
39                Ocean floor / ed. by Hamdy Bolles. --
0 3               New York : Bagsby, 1980.
                  540 p.
```

Connective added entry (set title)

```
QE                Oceans, v. 2
39                Ocean floor / ed. by Hamdy Bolles. --
0 3               New York : Bagsby, 1980.
                  540 p.
```

EXAMPLE 11 (cont.)

Author & title work analytic

```
QE              Ewing, Thomas.   Structure of the Gulf of
39              Mexico, in
0 3          Ocean floor / ed. by Hamdy Bolles. --
                New York . Bagsby, 1980.
                540 p.
```

Shelf list card

```
QE
39              Ocean floor / ed. by Hamdy Bolles. --
0 3              New York : Bagsby, 1980.
                540 p.




(space for housekeeping information)
```

EXAMPLE 12

An item of type 5 -- a set of books wherein each has its own distinctive title. The item is here cataloged under the set description principle. One work analytic has been made for one of the essays contained in volume 2. Book analytics have been made for the three component volumes. Compare with example 11.

Main entry

```
GC
57              Oceans / ed. by Hamdy Bolles. --
0 3                 New York : Bagsby, 1980.
                    3 v.

                    Contents: v.1. Sea water -- v.2. Ocean
                    floor -- v.3. Ocean currents


1. OCEANOGRAPHY.  I. Bolles, Hamdy, ed.  II., III., and
IV. Title analytics as in contents note.  V. Ewing, Thomas.
Structure of the Gulf of Mexico, in v.2 of
```

Subject added entry

```
GC              OCEANOGRAPHY
57              Oceans / ed. by Hamdy Bolles. --
0 3                 New York : Bagsby, 1980.
                    3 v.
```

EXAMPLE 12 (cont.)

Author added entry

```
GC              Bolles, Hamdy, ed.
57              Oceans / ed. by Hamdy Bolles. --
0 3             New York : Bagsby, 1980.
                3 v.
```

First book analytic

```
GC              Sea water, v.1 of
57              Oceans / ed. by Hamdy Bolles. --
0 3             New York : Bagsby, 1980.
                3 v.
```

EXAMPLE 12 (cont.)

Second book analytic

```
GC              Ocean floor, v.2 of
57              Oceans / ed. by Hamdy Bolles. --
0 3             New York : Bagsby, 1980.
                3 v.
```

Third book analytic

```
GC              Ocean currents, v.3 of
57              Oceans / ed. by Hamdy Bolles. --
0 3             New York : Bagsby, 1980.
                3 v.
```

EXAMPLE 12 (cont.)

Author & title work analytic

```
GC              Ewing, Thomas.  Structure of the Gulf of
57              Mexico, in v.2 of
0 3             Oceans / ed. Hamdy Bolles. --
                New York : Bagsby, 1980.
                3 v.
```

Shelf list card

```
GC
57              Oceans / ed. by Hamdy Bolles. --
0 3                New York : Bagsby, 1980.
                   3 v.




                (space for housekeeping information)
```

EXAMPLE 13

A kit consisting of five pieces, only one author traced.

Main entry

```
Audio
LIT          Living poetry of all peoples / selected
L5               by Joe Doe ; photographed by Hank Glick ;
                 narrated by Jocelyn Brown. -- Riverside :
                 Jones Media Productions, 1984.

                 Kit consisting of 2 cassettes, 1 filmstrip,
                 2 booklets.


1. POETRY.   I. Doe, Joe.
```


Author added entry

```
Audio        Doe, Joe.
LIT          Living poetry of all peoples / selected
L5               by Joe Doe ; photographed by Hank Glick ;
                 narrated by Jocelyn Brown. -- Riverside :
             Jones Media Productions, 1984.
             Kit consisting of 2 cassettes, 1 filmstrip,
             2 booklets.
```

EXAMPLE 13 (cont.)

Genre added entry

```
Audio         POETRY
LIT           Living poetry of all peoples / selected
L5               by Joe Doe ; photographed by Hank Glick ;
                 narrated by Jocelyn Brown. -- Riverside :
                 Jones Media Productions, 1984.

                 Kit consisting of 2 cassettes, 1 filmstrip,
                 2 booklets.
```


Shelf list card

```
Audio
LIT           Living poetry of all peoples / selected
L5               by Joe Doe ; photographed by Hank Glick ;
                 narrated by Jocelyn Brown. -- Riverside :
                 Jones Media Productions, 1984.
                 Kit consisting of 2 cassettes, 1 filmstrip,
                 2 booklets.


(space for housekeeping information)
```

Appendix B

USING OTHER LIBRARIES'
CATALOGING _____

For many books one can buy ready-made printed catalog cards
for less money than it would cost to type them "from scratch."
The chief supplier of printed cards in America is the Cataloging Distribution Service, Library of Congress, Washington,
DC   20541.

The Library of Congress card is indented in a more
complicated way and the entry principle varies.   But the LC
card is easily interfiled in the small library's catalog.   The
cards may look different, but no access points are missed.
When all added entries are made there will be subject entries,
title entries, and author entries, as in the example that follows.

Main entry

```
016.3613
B6       Blank, Marion.
              Working with people : a selected social casework bibliography
          / Compiled by Marion S. Blank. — 2nd ed. — New York :
          Family Service Association of America, ₍1981₎

              335 p. 23 cm.
              ISBN 0-87304-161-5




              1. Social case work—Bibliography.   I. Title.
              Z7164.C4B6   1981          016.3613'2—dc19       81-43789
              ₍HV43₎                       AACR 2   MARC CIP 12/81

          Library of Congress
```

First subject added entry

016.3613   SOCIAL CASE WORK--BIBLIOGRAPHY
B6   **Blank, Marion.**
                 Working with people : a selected social casework bibliography
            / Compiled by Marion S. Blank. — 2nd ed. — New York :
            Family Service Association of America, ₁1981₁

                335 p. 23 cm.
                ISBN 0-87304-161-5

                1. Social case work—Bibliography.   I. Title.
                Z7164.C4B6   1981   016.3613′2—dc19   81-43789
                ₁HV43₁   AACR 2   MARC CIP 12/81

                Library of Congress

Title added entry

016.3613   Working with people
B6   **Blank, Marion.**
                 Working with people : a selected social casework bibliography
            / Compiled by Marion S. Blank. — 2nd ed. — New York :
            Family Service Association of America, ₁1981₁

                335 p. 23 cm.
                ISBN 0-87304-161-5

                1. Social case work—Bibliography.   I. Title.
                Z7164.C4B6 . 1981   016.3613′2—dc19   81-43789
                ₁HV43₁   AACR 2   MARC CIP 12/81

                Library of Congress

Shelf list card

```
016.3613
B6      Blank, Marion.
           Working with people : a selected social casework bibliography
        / Compiled by Marion S. Blank. — 2nd ed. — New York :
        Family Service Association of America, ₍1981₎

           335  p.  23 cm.
           ISBN 0-87304-161-5

(space for housekeeping information)


           1. Social case work—Bibliography.    I. Title.
           Z7164.C4B6   1981              016.3613'2—dc19        81-43789
           ₍HV43₎                                   AACR 2   MARC CIP 12/81

           Library of Congress
```

The reader will notice several numbers on this Library
of Congress card. They are the international standard book
number, or ISBN (a book trade code that designates country
[0 for Great Britain and USA], then publisher [87304 for
Family Service Association of America] and book [161 for
Working with People]); the Library of Congress call number
(Z7164.C4B6 1981); the Dewey Decimal classification number
(016.3613'2--dc19); and the Library of Congress card number
(81-43789).

*   *   *

To emphasize the difference between cards made according to SMALL LIBRARY CATALOGING instructions and those
made by the Library of Congress, the following pages show
the main entries for some of the examples of Appendix A,
retyped the way they would appear in Library of Congress
style.

(Example 2, page 158)

```
692.1
W2          Wallach, Paul I.
                 Reading construction drawings / Paul
            I. Wallach ; Donald E. Hepler. -- New
            York : McGraw-Hill, 1981.
                 313 p.



                 1. Specification Writing.  2. Building--
            Contracts and Specifications.  I. Hepler,
            Donald E.  II. Title.
```

(Example 5, page 166)

```
574.19
P6          Advanced Institute of Photoreception,
                 Versilia, Italy, 1979.
                 Photoreception and sensory transduction /
            edited by Francesco Lenci and Giuliano
            Colombetti. -- New York : Planor Press,
            1980.
                 ix, 422 p. : ill. ; 26 cm.  (Advanced
            Institute series : Series A ; v. 33)

                              (continued on next card)
```

(Example 5--cont.)

```
574.19
P6            Advanced Institute of Photoreception...
                  card 2


              Papers presented at the Advanced Institute
         of Photoreception, Versilia, Italy, 1979.

              1. Photoreceptors--Congresses. 2. Senses
         and Sensation--Congresses. I. Lenci, Fran-
         cesco. II. Colombetti, Giuliano.  III. Title

QH515.N22 1979                              80-12345678
```

(Example 9, page 178)

```
         Journal of Earth. -- Vol. 1, no. 1
           (1984)-          . -- New York :
         American Earth Society, 1984-
              v. ; 20 cm.

         Quarterly.




         I. American Earth Society.
```

Many new books today carry what is known as "Cataloging in Publication," or CIP: catalog card information generated on the basis of galley proofs submitted to the Library of Congress and printed on the back, or verso, of the title page. Here is an example taken from a recent publication:

Beakley, George C.
  Design: serving the needs of man.

  Based on the author's Introduction to engineering design and graphics.
    1. Engineering design.   I. Chilton, Ernest G., joint author.   II. Title.
  TA174.B39   620.0042   73-2762
  ISBN 0-02-307240-7

When a book like this is bought for a small library, the CIP information can be used to generate a deck of cards. Imprint and physical description must be taken from the book itself. Following are the cards based on the example given above.

Main entry

620
D4   Design : serving the needs of man /
                George C. Beakley and Ernest G.
                Chilton. -- New York : Macmillan,
                1974.
                546 p.

1. ENGINEERING DESIGN.   I. Beakley, George C.
II. Chilton, Ernest G.

Subject added entry

```
620              ENGINEERING DESIGN
D4               Design : serving the needs ofman /
                 George C. Beakley and Ernest G.
                 Chilton. -- New York : Macmillan,
                 1974.
                 546 p.
```

First author added entry

```
620              Beakley, George C.
D4               Design : serving the needs of man /
                 George C. Beakley and Ernest G.
                 Chilton. -- New York : Macmillan,
                 1974.
                 546 p.
```

Second author added entry

```
620          Chilton, Ernest G.
D4           Design : serving the needs of man /
             George C. Beakley and Ernest G.
             Chilton. -- New York : Macmillan,
             1974.
             546 p.
```

Shelf list card

```
620
D4           Design : serving the needs of man /
             George C. Beakley and Ernest G.
             Chilton. -- New York : Macmillan,
             1974.
             546 p.


(space for housekeeping information)
```

Cataloging information can also be taken from entries in printed bibliographic aids such as the Weekly Record or the American Book Publishing Record. Here is an example for a book of type 1 from the Weekly Record:

This information can be used to generate the following cards:

Main entry

688.6
A8
        ARNOLD, James.   688.6
        All drawn by horses / James Arnold. Newton
        Abbot [Eng.] ; North Pomfret, Vt. : David &
        Charles, c1979. 142 p. : ill. ; 24 x 26 cm.
        Includes index. [TS2010.A68] 79-318912 ISBN
        0-7153-7682-9 : 22.00
        1. Carriages and carts—Great Britain—History. I.
        Title.

1.CARRIAGES AND CARTS--GREAT BRITAIN--HISTORY.
I. Arnold, James.

Subject added entry

```
688.6            CARRIAGES AND CARTS--GREAT BRITAIN--HISTORY
A8               All drawn by horses / James Arnold. --
                 North Pomfret, VT : David and Charles,
                 1979.
                 142 p.
```

Author added entry

```
688.6            Arnold, James
A8               All drawn by horses / James Arnold. --
                 North Pomfret, VT : David and Charles,
                 1979.
                 142 p.
```

Shelf list card

```
688.6
A8          All drawn by horses / James Arnold. --
            North Pomfret, VT : David and Charles,
            1979.
            142 p.



(space for housekeeping information)



```

        Lately a number of computer-stored bibliographic utilities
have become widely available. Libraries with access to the
best known of these, the OCLC online union catalog, are not
likely to type their own cards. But many small libraries may
be connected by computer terminal to the files of the DIALOG
Information Services Inc. Such libraries can now query the
Library of Congress Machine Readable Cataloging (MARC) and
Retrospective Machine Readable (REMARC) databases for cataloging information. REMARC is a file of bibliographic records
consisting, essentially, of Library of Congress cards for older
books. Here is a sample REMARC record as it would be displayed on the screen of the library's computer terminal connected by telephone to the DIALOG computer in Palo Alto,
California:

        The Bentley Ballads
        Doran, John, 1807-1878 ed.
        London, R. Bentley, 1862 ix, 452p. 18 cm.
        Place of publication: England
        LCCN: 12025305
        LC: PR 1175.B45
        Languages: English
        Document type: Monograph
        Descriptors: English poetry 19th and 20th
     century; English ballads and songs.

In a small library this information can be used to produce catalog cards:

Main entry

```
821
B3          Bentley ballads / ed. by John Doran. --
               London : R. Bentley, 1862.
               452 p.




            1. ENGLISH BALLADS AND SONGS.   I Doran, John, ed.
```

Categorical added entry (a genre entry)

```
821              ENGLISH BALLADS AND SONGS
B3          Bentley ballads / ed. by John Doran. --
               London : R. Bentley, 1862.
               452 p.
```

Note that in traditional library terminology this would be called a subject added entry, although the book is probably not a book about ballads but a book containing ballads.

Author added entry

```
821          Doran, John, ed.
B3           Bentley ballads / ed. by John Doran. --
             London : R. Bentley, 1862.
             452 p.




```

Shelf list card

```
821
B3           Bentley ballads / ed. by John Doran. --
             London : R. Bentley, 1862.
             452 p.



(space for housekeeping information...)


```

Inside the computer, incidentally, the bibliographic information is stored in the MARC format. In this format every element of the description is given a field name and a numeric field "tag." Thus the Library of Congress call number is stored in a field tagged "050"; the title field is tagged "245"; and so forth. Here is the same REMARC record used above, this time displayed with MARC tags (i.e., in DIALOG format 4):

```
008:  810428S1862
010:  12025305
050:  PR1175.B45
130:  BENTLEY'S MISCELLANY
245:  THE BENTLEY BALLADS
260:  LONDON, R. BENTLEY
300:  IX, 452 P.   18 CM.
650:  ENGLISH BALLADS AND SONGS;
      ENGLISH POETRY--19TH AND 20TH CENTURY
700:  DORAN, JOHN, 1807-1878, ED.
```

The entire body of the MARC format is explained in a manual of formidable proportions. Nobody appointed to run a small library needs to be much concerned about the format. However, it does help when one recognizes a few key tags. In the sample DIALOG display above, for example, it is immediately obvious to the initiate that what follows 245 is the title of the item and that tag 650 shows the subject headings assigned, while tag 700 gives the name of the person for whom an added entry must be made.

This last example also shows that one can never rely entirely on other libraries' cataloging, not even if stored in a computer. Clearly, a book such as The Bentley Ballads, published in 1862, can hardly be expected to contain any twentieth-century poetry. Yet this is what one of the headings in the computerized version (tag 650) would make us believe.

Appendix C

LIBRARIAN'S HELPER: A SIMPLE WAY TO
WRITE CATALOG CARDS BY COMPUTER _____

Catalog cards can be produced on a personal computer. The
advantage of this method is that the cataloging information
needs to be keyed in only once. Additional cards can be
generated by the computer from that one basic record as
needed.

It is impossible to write down a generally applicable procedure for computer-generated cataloging because no two readers will have the same equipment or software. What is offered
here, instead, is a brief sketch of one simple card writing
program, Librarian's Helper: A Productivity Tool for Librarians, by Jennifer Pritchett and Fred Hill, Version 4.0 (Metuch-
en: Scarecrow Press, 1986). This is available from about
$200, price depending on hardware and operating system to
be used. It comes with a 30-page manual that is exceptionally
easy to read and follow. The program runs on Apple, IBM
PC (or compatible), and other machines. It requires a printer
with a vertical forms tractor.

Librarian's Helper is a menu-driven program. The user
is prompted step by step through the process of building one
catalog record at a time. When all the data for one book have
been entered into the computer, the program allows the user
to inspect the cards on the screen and make corrections if
needed. When all cards for that book are found to be correct,
they are printed out and another book can be started. The
program also prints labels from the same input.

Librarian's Helper was designed to print catalog cards

205

in the traditional layout, accommodating different entry principles. But the program can very easily be adapted to print
title main entry cards very similar to those shown in this
book. It takes only a few special steps during data input.
Here are the input prompts that Librarian's Helper presents.
For each we suggest what the cataloger should do.

Author   Ignore this prompt. It is used only for so-
                        called author main entries.

Title proper   Enter the title, or the part that precedes
                        the subtitle.

Subtitle   Enter the subtitle, if present.

Parallel title   Used only rarely, when there is a title in
                        another language.

Uniform title   Ignore this prompt. It is used only for
                        uniform title main entries and for certain
                        author main entries. See also below, Added
                        entries.

Statement of   Enter here the name(s) of the author(s).
responsibility

Subsequent   Used only rarely if there is another person
statement of   or group performing a different function
responsibility   (e.g., translator as opposed to author).

Edition   Used only when the book is not a first edi-
                        tion.

Material   Used only for certain non-book items. Can
specific   safely be ignored in a small library.
details

Place of   Enter city, usually first mentioned American
publication   city only if published in the United States.

Publisher   Enter name of publisher.

Date   Enter latest copyright date.

Call # 1-5   Enter up to 5 lines of call number.

Series note   Enter title of series to which the book be-
                     longs, if applicable.

Tracings   This actually means "subject headings."
                     Enter subject headings, in capital letters.

Analytical   This actually means "analytical added entry
entries   headings." Up to ten title/author pairs can
                     be entered here.

Added   This actually means "added entry headings
entries   other than subject headings." To enter data
                     in this field begin by clearing the field
                     (option 1, "re-enter line 1"). This removes
                     the preprogrammed "1. Title" phrase. You
                     are now ready to enter author added entry
                     headings. Just type the name(s) as they are
                     to appear in the heading (eg., "Doe, Joe").
                     If a title added entry is needed, enter it
                     here, beginning with the word "Title:."
                     Note that there is a space after the colon.
                     If a uniform title added entry heading is
                     needed, type it enclosed in brackets after
                     "Title:."

ISBN   Enter ISBN. Can safely be ignored in small
                     libraries.

Library of   Enter Library of Congress card number.
Congress   Can safely be ignored in small libraries.
number

Extent of   Enter here number of pages, volumes, units,
item   etc. (e.g., "2 cassettes").

Other   Enter here a note that the book is illustrated
physical   or similar information. Can safely be ignored
details   in small libraries.

Dimensions   Enter here height of book or notes concerning
and accom-   media (e.g., "stereo, 12 in").
panying
materials

Note   Up to four paragraphs of notes can be en-
paragraphs   tered. Use for any important data that do
                        not fit elsewhere.

Shelf card   Enter housekeeping information. Can also
information   be omitted and entered later by hand.

When these prompts are answered in the manner suggested, the result will be a perfect set of title main entry
catalog cards. After a few practice sessions the program user
will become quite efficient and produce high quality cards,
error free, at a rate that would be unattainable on a regular
typewriter.

Note that printers producing catalog cards have a
tendency to "hang up" and "eat cards." One type of card
stock that we have found very satisfactory is University
Products' medium weight, LC cream, continuous catalog card,
stock number 304-P135.

Appendix D

LIBRARY SUPPLIES AND EQUIPMENT _____

Wherever books and other publications are cataloged and pre-
pared for use, certain supplies and equipment are needed.
Several nationwide distributors specialize in this market.
Here are the addresses of the best known among them:

> BRO-DART
> 1609 Memorial Ave.
> Williamsport, PA   17705
>
> DEMCO Educational Corp.
> Box 7488
> Madison, WI   53707
>
> GAYLORD Bros., Inc.
> Box 4901
> Syracuse, NY   13221
>
> HIGHSMITH Co., Inc.
> Box 800
> Fort Atkinson, WI   53538-0800
>
> UNIVERSITY PRODUCTS, Inc.
> Box 101
> Holyoke, MA   01041

These firms issue profusely illustrated catalogs that contain
a good bit of practical, technical information.

Here is a selected list of some of the things a small
library might require:

Accession sheets
Adhesive tape
Adhesives ("Library Paste")
Book cards and pockets for check-out
Book covers, clear plastic
Card catalog cabinet
Card sorter
Cassette albums
Catalog cards, 7.5 x 12.5 cm
Catalog cards, continuous form, pin fed
Catalog guide cards
Charging trays
Charging tray guides
Dictionary stand
Electric eraser
Erasing fluid or tape
Marking stylus
Message labels (e.g., "For Room Use")
Microfilm storage cabinet
Pamphlet binders
Paper cutter
Periodical checking cards
Princeton files
Rubber stamps
Self-adhesive labels
Sign maker
Slide sorter
Stapler, heavy duty
Typewriter with card holder (to prevent smearing of
    cards when typing near the edge)
Visible record cabinet for periodical checking cards